Lois Lowry

Other titles in the *Authors Teens Love* series:

Ray Bradbury
*Master of Science Fiction
and Fantasy*
ISBN-13: 978-0-7660-2240-9
ISBN-10: 0-7660-2240-4

Gary Paulsen
*Voice of Adventure
and Survival*
ISBN-13: 978-0-7660-2721-3
ISBN-10: 0-7660-2721-X

Orson Scott Card
Architect of Alternate Worlds
ISBN-13: 978-0-7660-2354-3
ISBN-10: 0-7660-2354-0

Philip Pullman
Master of Fantasy
ISBN-13: 978-0-7660-2447-2
ISBN-10: 0-7660-2447-4

Roald Dahl
Author of Charlie and the
Chocolate Factory
ISBN-13: 978-0-7660-2353-6
ISBN-10: 0-7660-2353-2

Jerry Spinelli
Master Teller of Teen Tales
ISBN-13: 978-0-7660-2718-3
ISBN-10: 0-7660-2718-X

Paula Danziger
Voice of Teen Troubles
ISBN-13: 978-0-7660-2444-1
ISBN-10: 0-7660-2444-X

R. L. Stine
*Creator of Creepy and
Spooky Stories*
ISBN-13: 978-0-7660-2445-8
ISBN-10: 0-7660-2445-8

C. S. Lewis
Chronicler of Narnia
ISBN-13: 978-0-7660-2446-5
ISBN-10: 0-7660-2446-6

J. R. R. Tolkien
Master of Imaginary Worlds
ISBN-13: 978-0-7660-2246-1
ISBN-10: 0-7660-2246-3

Joan Lowery Nixon
Masterful Mystery Writer
ISBN-13: 978-0-7660-2194-5
ISBN-10: 0-7660-2194-7

E. B. White
Spinner of Webs and Tales
ISBN-13: 978-0-7660-2350-5
ISBN-10: 0-7660-2350-8

Lois Lowry

The Giver of Stories and Memories

Lisa Rondinelli Albert

Enslow Publishers, Inc.
40 Industrial Road
Box 398
Berkeley Heights, NJ 07922
USA

http://www.enslow.com

Acknowledgments

Sincere gratitude to Lois Lowry for her generosity of time and photographs, and for her outstanding contributions to children's literature.

Special thanks to the members of my talented critique groups, especially Candie Moonshower, who was my second set of eyes.

To my husband Joe, and my children, Joe and Alexandra, for their confidence and support, I am eternally grateful.

Library of Congress Cataloging-in-Publication Data

Albert, Lisa Rondinelli.
    Lois Lowry : the giver of stories and memories / by Lisa Rondinelli Albert.
        p. cm. — (Authors teens love)
    Includes bibliographical references and index.
    ISBN-13: 978-0-7660-2722-0
    ISBN-10: 0-7660-2722-8
    1. Lowry, Lois—Juvenile literature. 2. Authors, American—20th century—Biography—Juvenile literature. 3. Young adult fiction—Authorship—Juvenile literature. I. Title.
    PS3562.O923Z54 2007
    813'.54—dc22
    [B]   2006034045

Printed in the United States of America

10 9 8 7 6 5 4 3 2 1

To Our Readers: We have done our best to make sure all Internet addresses in this book were active and appropriate when we went to press. However, the author and publisher have no control over and assume no liability for the material available on those Internet sites or on other Web sites they may link to. Any comments or suggestions can be sent by e-mail to comments@enslow.com or to the address on the back cover.

Cover Illustration: All interior photos courtesy of Lois Lowry, except pp. 6, 100, photo by William Goldstein, courtesy of Lois Lowry; and p. 91, photo by Dianne L. Peterson.

Photos and Illustrations: Photo courtesy of Lois Lowry (foreground); Carl Feryok (background art).

Contents

Chapter 1

Hunting Crows

It was a fall morning in 1975 when thirty-eight-year-old Lois Lowry woke to the smell of dry leaves and late apples. The smell in the air brought a memory of a similar November day when she was nine and went crow hunting with her father.[1]

With the memory fresh in mind, Lowry sat down and wrote a story about that day. It began with the words "It was morning, early, barely light, cold for November. I was nine and the war was over. At home, in the bed next to mine, my older sister still slept, adolescent, her blonde hair streaming over the edge of the sheet. I sat shyly in the front seat of the car next to the stranger who was my father."[2]

The story was short and in it, nine-year-old Lois is given a crow call—a little wooden instrument that makes the sound of a crow when blown into. Lois is to blow the call when told to by her father, and when the crows rise out of the trees, he will shoot them. She is terrified but when her father gives her a nod, Lois puts the call to her mouth and blows. Crows fly out of the trees and the air fills with noise. When there is no sound of a gun, Lois turns to see that her father has laid his gun against a rock. He is simply watching her and smiling.[3]

Using her memory, Lowry was able to fashion that event into a story. Even though it appears to be about hunting crows, it tells a deeper story about a child and her father, who both wanted to love each other, and who both made sacrifices so that could happen.

Shortly after "Crow Call" was published in *Redbook Magazine* in December 1975, Lowry received an interesting letter from Melanie Kroupa, an editor. Kroupa worked for Houghton Mifflin, a well-known publisher of children's literature, and she wrote to Lowry to ask her if she had ever considered writing for kids.[4]

Up until that point, Lowry's writing had appeared in several newspapers and magazines. She had also written two textbooks for an educational publisher. Although this type of writing paid her bills, Lowry realized she had not reached the place she needed to go.[5] So the idea of writing books for children interested Lowry a lot. About this time, her marriage was ending and for the first time in her life, she would have to earn a living and make her way alone.

It was not until she went back and opened the doors of her past that she knew she should write for children. Digging through her childhood memories and emotions, Lowry began her journey of creating stories for children. "Everything a writer experiences as a young person goes into the later writing in some form," Lowry has said.[6] She was thirty-nine by the time she wrote her first children's book, *A Summer to Die*, a fictionalized story about the early death of her sister, Helen. This would not be the last time Lowry would use her past experiences to create a story.

Lowry's ability to recollect her childhood was so incredible that she was able to remember specific details of a day back when she was only three years old. Simply by looking at an old photograph of herself and Helen standing with a clown, parts of the day they had spent at the World's Fair in 1940 unraveled in her mind. "I look back now at photographs and see myself, wide-eyed at three, peering shyly at a clown who has apparently happened along and paused to speak to the two little blonde girls standing beside their mother. But I don't remember the clown with the wide grease-paint smile."[7]

Even though she did not recall the clown, seeing the photograph brought back other memories: ". . . apparently I must remember those dresses, even now, close to fifty years later, because although the photographs are black and white, I can see in my mind the blue of Helen's pinafore, and the slightly darker blue of my little cotton jacket, the red and blue plaid of my skirt. I can remember the colors."

Then, on what she believes was the same day, Lowry had an experience that ingrained itself into her mind forever. The experience created a memory filled with emotion and feeling instead of one with visuals, sounds, or touch. Alone in a dim corner, three-year-old Lois danced and twirled, holding her parasol above her. She whirled around and around in a circle until she became dizzy.

"I remember the happy blur of it. Something crashes. Shatters. And the blur of ecstasy is gone in an instant, supplanted by horror, humiliation. The parasol, whirling, has hit something: one of the fragile elegant objects." Young Lois hid her face against her father's shoulder and cried. "I think it is my first memory, this combination of ecstasy, humiliation, the futility of comfort."[8]

> **"Everything a writer experiences . . . goes into the later writing."**
>
> **—Lois Lowry**

Even though family surrounded her, Lois was a solitary child who lived in a world of books and her own imagination. She was reading at the age of three and creating stories in her mind not long after that. When she was eight, her Aunt Kate allowed Lois to play with a very expensive antique doll. It was an exquisite baby doll with a hand-painted china head and fancy clothes.

As Lois played with the doll on the huge old porch at Aunt Kate's house, she made up stories. They were not the typical pretend stories of an eight-year-old child. Her imagination was extraordinary and her make-believe included long, dramatic scenes.

Enchanted with the doll, Lois's story began, "The sunlight fell across the young girl's arm as she rocked, cradling the delicate infant . . ."[9]

Aunt Kate let Lois take the doll home for a visit. It was not hers to keep, but she still cherished it as if it were her own. During the doll visit, Lois's little brother, who was just a toddler at the time, gleefully grabbed at the doll. He threw it to the floor, shattering its china head into pieces. Even though she was heartbroken, Lois continued to imagine the doll's make-believe life and tragic end. "The brutal stranger wrest the infant from her helpless arms . . ."[10]

Dramatic, yes, and an early sign of the writer Lois would grow up to become. Her uncanny ability to recall childhood events, along with her knack for telling stories, would lead her to create books like no other and become a two-time Newbery award-winning author.

Chapter 2

The Middle Child

It was March 20, 1937, when blonde-haired, blue-eyed Lois was born in Hawaii on the island of Oahu. Originally, Lois was given the name Cena, after her Norwegian grandmother, but after her grandmother was notified, she announced that no grandchild of hers should bear that name. That announcement came by way of a telegram in which her grandmother insisted that her new grandchild be given an American name. The name was quickly changed to honor two of her aunts, and from then on, she would be called Lois Ann.[1] Lois Ann Hammersberg was the second daughter of Robert and Katharine Hammersberg.

Robert Hammersberg was an Army dentist and a fine photographer who also collected cameras. The first photograph he snapped of Lois was taken when she was just a squirming newborn at thirty-six-hours old. All the images Robert captured and developed in his darkroom are treasured to this day by Lois and her family.

Even though his military life and photography kept him busy, Robert Hammersberg always made time to be a loving and attentive father. As Lois grew, he would make her laugh by speaking in his family's funny-sounding Norwegian language, with its lilting inflection. Lois would squeal with delight at one story in particular, a story he told about eating lutefisk, a pickled fish. It was not just the words he used to tell the tale that made Lois giggle, but the expressions on his face. He would wrinkle his face to show excruciating disgust when he described the taste of the lutefisk. Even though he insisted he loved to eat it, his exaggerated face showed the true flavor of the fish and made for an entertaining story.[2]

Lois also heard her father's boyhood stories about riding horseback along a river in La Crosse, Wisconsin, and about the fact that his family name was originally Anderson, not Hammersberg. When Robert's parents came to the United States from Norway, their last name was Anderson until the paymaster on the railroad asked them to change it. Apparently, too many immigrants had had that name and it was simply too confusing. Carl and Cena Anderson decided to take the name Hammersberg after the Norwegian village they had come from.[3]

Carl Hammersberg died while Robert was very

young so he was never a part of Lois's life. However, Cena Hammersberg was very much a part of Lois's childhood and she was called "Nonny" instead of grandma. Nonny was very talented at making doll clothes for Lois to play with. The fragile lace and tiny hand-stitched hems were magnificent and envied by all Lois's friends.[4]

Lois's mother, Katharine Hammersberg, doted on her daughters. It is evident from all the photographs taken by her husband that Katharine enjoyed dressing her girls in fancy dresses. In fact, Katharine was picking out clothing for her children even before she had them. She was twenty-two years old when she spent the summer of 1928 traveling to European countries where she bought little foreign outfits for her future children to wear.[5]

In 1945, with her youngest daughter now the right size to wear one of these outfits, Katharine dressed eight-year-old Lois in the lederhosen she had brought back from Switzerland. With his camera ready, Lois's father snapped a picture of her modeling the short leather pants with suspenders, the thick wool socks, and a hat with a feather in it. That photograph of Lois shows her as an adorable little girl with an embarrassed expression on her face. Her head tilts to one side and her mouth curls in disgust as she poses in the *boys'* lederhosen.[6]

Katharine grew up in the town of Carlisle, Pennsylvania, where her father, Merkel Landis, was a bank president and an attorney. Her ancestors had been lawyers and farmers generations before. She met her future husband, Robert, while he was stationed with the Army at Carlisle Barracks.

In 1935, while Robert Hammersberg was stationed at Fort Benning in Georgia, Katharine gave birth to their first child, Helen. Their stay in Georgia lasted only a short time, and in the fall of 1936, the family of three moved to Hawaii.[7] This would be the first of many moves to come, but it was their first across the Pacific Ocean. Katharine was pregnant with their second child during this move, and in the spring of 1937, Lois was born.

When Lois was baptized in Hawaii at the age of eleven months, she wore a tiny lei of Hawaiian flowers around her neck.[8] Helen was three years older than Lois, and from early on, the sisters were always well dressed in outfits that Katharine had pressed and starched.

Lois spent the first couple years of her life in Honolulu, Hawaii, where lush tropical gardens and beaches were her playlands. In a scene recorded by her father using his movie camera, two-year-old Lois is in the garden outside her home. She is wearing a blue dress and holding a watering can that is almost as big as she is, and, as she tilts the watering can, a dribble waters the hibiscus flowers.[9]

The days she spent at the beach at Waikiki would not last long, though. Being a child of a military officer meant there would be a lot of moving for Lois and her family. All the warm days and sunshine of Hawaii would soon be replaced with

Lois and her sister, Helen, with their mother in 1939.

big city noise, crowded streets, and cold. The family was moving to New York.

As most toddlers would, Lois whimpered about the long ocean voyage through the Panama Canal. She wanted to go back home to the rainbows and flowers of Honolulu. During the journey, she trembled and whined to her mother about the cold and the wind. Her mother tried to explain that "home" was not a permanent thing.[10]

The Hammersbergs settled into an apartment in Brooklyn, New York, and it did not take long for Lois to feel at home. Lois's father gave her reproduction military dog tags to wear. He had the gold engraved with their New York address: 140 87th Street.

Reading and books became an important part of Lois's life. Her mother had read to her often, but it was her sister, Helen, who played a major part in Lois's learning to read. When Helen would return home from school with her books and attempt to do her homework, Lois would hang on her arm and distract her. Helen then explained the process of reading in a methodical, matter-of-fact way.[11]

Lois learned that the letters had sounds, and when the sounds were put together, they formed words. After that, when Helen was gone each day, Lois studied books. She carefully looked at the stories she already knew by heart and taught herself which sounds went with each letter.[12]

A favorite book of hers was about a turtle named Humphrey and, as a new reader, figuring

Lois's reproduction dog tags, given to her by her father shortly after the family moved from Hawaii to New York.

out the "ph" sound gave her some trouble. She also read a set of books called My Bookhouse. The first book had a long poem about an old, old, old woman and a boy who was just past three. Lois loved that poem so much she memorized it.[13]

By the time she entered nursery school when she was three, Lois was already reading and writing on her own. One day, her nursery school teacher sent a note home to her mother that read: "She refuses to drink her milk at snack time and her unusual ability to read sets her apart from the other children."[14] This message was not meant as a compliment. The teacher sent the note out of concern because Lois would rather sit in a corner and read a book than play games with the class.

When the children in her class marched around, swaying their arms in front of them and pretending to be elephants, Lois refused. She was embarrassed by the silly play and retreated to a corner to read instead. Even at this early age, Lois had a sense of her individuality and enjoyed watching instead of participating. She was a precocious child who was quite aware that her reading skills set her apart. But that did not bother her.

Later in her adult life, Lois would reflect on her preschool days and admit that her three-year-old self was a bit of an intellectual snob.[15] She also recognized that her desire to be an observer at such an early age somehow contributed to her becoming a writer.[16]

Lois's keen observation skills and her ability to read fed her mind. Her mother recognized that Lois's imagination, curiosity, and love of words were part of her personality. She nurtured it by providing books, writing materials, and privacy.

On December 7, 1941, several new words became part of Lois's vocabulary: World War II, Pearl Harbor, and uniform. Lois's mother had been in the kitchen listening to the radio when the announcement came across the airwaves. Lois got frightened as she watched her mother's face, so she ran to her father. "Pearl Harbor is on the radio, Daddy," she told him, "and Mama is crying." To Lois, the words "Pearl Harbor" reminded her of a lady's name because she knew a woman named Pearl from the grocery store on the corner.[17]

Lois was four and a half years old when Japan bombed the United States Naval Base at Pearl Harbor in Hawaii. She was probably too young to fully understand what the enemy attack was all about. She did understand, though, that because of Pearl Harbor, her father had to wear his military uniform instead of regular, civilian clothes.[18] Part of his uniform included a military hat that he would allow Lois to wear in their house. She liked to march around their Brooklyn, New York, apartment while wearing her pajamas and her daddy's special hat.[19]

Seeing her father in his Army uniform every day was just one change the war brought to Lois's life. When Lois began kindergarten in 1942, her sister, Helen, was in third grade. At school in New York, children practiced what to do in the event of an enemy attack. During these air raid drills, all the schoolchildren would run to a subway station and hide from pretend bombs. As the children hid during the mock emergency, Helen would find Lois and hold her hand. With ribbons in their hair and the dog tags around their necks, the sisters waited underground for the drill to be over.[20]

There were many changes at her home and school. Lois was often told that these changes were "because of the war." It seemed to be the answer for everything.[21] Because of the war, Lois's father was called on to serve his country, and he was sent overseas to the Pacific. Because of the war, Lois's family moved again, but this time, it was without her father.

Chapter 3

On the Move

After her father was sent off to war, Lois, Helen, and their mother moved to Pennsylvania. The noisy big city to which Lois was accustomed was replaced with a quiet town called Carlisle.[1] In place of the New York apartment was now a large brick house with a grand staircase, fireplaces, and a library.

Lois's grandparents, Merkel and Mary Landis, owned the big home. Grandpa Landis was a loving person who spent time reading to Lois when he was not busy at his bank. Grandma Landis was Lois's step-grandmother and she was far less affectionate.

Shortly after the family moved in with Grandpa and Grandma, a new member of the Hammersberg family arrived. Lois's baby brother, Jon, was born.

A telegram announcing the news of the baby boy was sent to Lois's father, who was still overseas. Jon had blue eyes and blonde hair just like his older sisters.

Becoming a big sister was another change for Lois. Her mother needed to spend a lot of time taking care of baby Jon. There were feedings, naps, drool, diapers, baths, and crying. And because Grandma Landis would become very nervous when she heard the baby's crying, Lois's mother spent a lot of time upstairs with the newborn.[2]

A lot of things made Grandma Landis nervous, and children in general were one of those things, Lois included. If she had an unbuckled shoe, an untied hair ribbon, or even a grass stain on her knee, Grandma would aim Lois toward a bathroom and tell her, "*March*, young lady." Lois would dutifully march and go clean up and make herself tidy again.[3]

A lot of Lois's time was spent alone because Helen was off with the new friends she had made and Lois was still too young to play outside by herself. Helen had more freedom since she was three years older. She was on the verge of adolescence, becoming a young lady, and she was no longer interested in playing games of tag with Lois. Her sister's newfound friends and time away made Lois feel resentful, envious, and sad.[4]

Lois often turned to reading to fill her time and for entertainment. The bedroom she shared with her sister had lots of books in it. In the evenings at bedtime, Lois and Helen would settle inside the

The Pennsylvania home of Lois's grandparents, the Landises.

room with its pale green flowered wallpaper and listen to their mother read. *Winnie the Pooh* and *Mr. Popper's Penguins* were two of Lois's favorites.[5]

But there were other books: leather-bound books in dark greens and crimsons with gold lettering embossed on them. To Lois, these books looked important and smelled of wisdom. She was drawn to them, but they were Grandpa Landis's books.[6]

Grandpa was an honorable, formal man with an important job, and Lois was in awe of him. He was well educated and a hard worker. It was Lois's grandpa, Merkel Landis, who invented the Christmas Savings Fund in 1910. It was a new way for bank customers to put money away into a savings account until it was needed at holiday time. He took his job very seriously and worked his way up to become a bank president.[7]

As a child, Lois probably did not know that her grandpa had played shortstop on his college baseball team, but she did know he liked to chew gum. In the evenings after dinner, Lois would watch him unwrap a stick of Black Jack gum and chew it slowly while he listened to the radio.

One evening, when Lois was five years old, Grandpa took her into his library.

The leather-bound books filled bookcases that lined the walls from floor to ceiling. Grandpa selected a volume of poetry, and, with Lois on his lap in his blue wing chair, he opened it ceremoniously.[8] He read a long poem with difficult words that Lois did not understand, but she listened to it

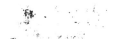

with fascination. Being chosen to join Grandpa in his library was special, especially since he had not invited Lois's sister. This was their time, and she enjoyed being on his lap, listening to the sound of the words.

There was a line in the poem that made Lois shiver when she heard it. It went:

> The speechless babe, and the gray-headed man—
> Shall one by one be gathered to thy side.

Lois related to this part because it made her think about her and her grandpa, together. To Lois, the speechless babe and the gray-headed man were them.[9]

Being chosen to join Grandpa in his library was special.

The pair returned to the library night after night, and Lois always asked to hear the same poem. She grew very fond of it and listened carefully for her favorite part. Soon, she was mouthing the words silently as her grandpa read aloud. Grandpa noticed that Lois was following along and he asked her if she knew the rest of the poem. When Lois recited the words all the way to the end, Grandpa said, "Remarkable."[10]

Grandpa was impressed with Lois's ability to memorize the long poem. One summer night when he was hosting a dinner party, he got her out of

Lois at eight years of age with her brother Jon, age two.

bed and held her hand as they walked down the stairs. Half asleep, Lois held on to her doll and followed her grandpa into the parlor where the guests had gathered.

On formal occasions such as this, the maids were required to wear their black uniforms with stiff white aprons.[11] They darted in and out of the swinging door that led to the kitchen as they served the guests. When Lois entered the parlor, wearing her pink pajamas with feet, Grandpa introduced her to women in gauzy summer dresses and men in suits and ties.[12]

Grandpa asked Lois to recite the poem for his guests and she obliged. As she stood on the Oriental rug, she closed her eyes to make believe she was invisible. Then, she recited all eighty-one lines of the poem, "Thanatopsis," by William Cullen Bryant, of which the final two paragraphs read:

> . . . As the long train
> Of ages glide away, the sons of men,
> The youth in life's green spring, and he who goes
> In the full strength of years, matron and maid,
> The speechless babe, and the gray-headed man—
> Shall one by one be gathered to thy side
> By those, who in their turn shall follow them.
>
> So live, that when thy summons comes to join
> The innumerable caravan which moves
> To that mysterious realm, where each shall take
> His chamber in the silent halls of death,
> Thou go not, like the quarry-slave at night,
> Scourged to his dungeon, but, sustained and soothed
> By an unfaltering trust, approach thy grave
> Like one who wraps the drapery of his couch
> About him, and lies down to pleasant dreams.[13]

Having the ability to memorize such a difficult poem was indeed remarkable for a five year old. Lois's love of words was being nurtured and apprcciated by her family, but her performance that evening also impressed one of her grandfather's guests. Edward MacFunn Biddle III was a dignified and quiet man. To Lois, he appeared to be an old man in a three-piece suit, but he was an important man. He was a judge, and his official name was The Honorable Edwin MacFunn Biddle III. Judge Biddle had something in common with Lois. Like Lois, he also had an excellent memory.[14]

> **Lois's love of words was being nurtured and appreciated by her family.**

The guests went back to their dinner party as Lois yawned and took her grandpa's hand. He led her back to her room and into her bed where she lay down to her own pleasant dreams.[15] She would not know until later in life just how big of an impression she made on Judge Biddle that night.

Besides her grandpa, Lois bonded with another person in the big house. Fleta Jordan was a nurturing woman who worked as a cook for Lois's grandparents. Known simply as The Cook, Fleta was the African-American lady in the kitchen who welcomed Lois into her world.[16]

Wearing her daytime uniform of blue with a white apron, Fleta let Lois hang around in the kitchen and watch her cook. Sometimes, Fleta would sprinkle cinnamon onto Lois's fingertips. She would also tell stories while Lois sat in a chair, listening and dangling her legs. Best of all, Fleta Jordan told Lois a secret.[17]

It seems Fleta understood Lois's need for human contact, and she also nurtured Lois's imagination by showing her the servants' staircase. It was a long, dark, narrow staircase that even her sister, Helen, did not know about.

By going through a door that was next to the refrigerator, Lois would disappear and almost magically, end up in the hall upstairs. Access to this special staircase made Lois feel powerful. It was not anything like the grand staircase in the main part of the house. That one was wide, with a tall clock on the landing, and when Lois climbed it, she was usually just going to bed.

But when Lois climbed her secret staircase, she could go anywhere her imagination would take her. With the top and bottom doors both closed, the staircase was pitch-black dark, and Lois played pretend and tested her courage. She let her imagination take over and made up stories. While hiding and shivering with terror she told herself, "The little girl was in a dark, dark place but she was very brave . . ."[18]

Having the staircase also meant Lois had a place to duck under cover and hide from her stern grandma. If Lois was upstairs and heard the sound of Grandma's footsteps, she would slip through a door next to the linen closet and flee. Her escape would lead her down to the kitchen where she was greeted with a knowing grin from Fleta.

Lois not only found a friend in Fleta, but also in Fleta's granddaughter, Gloria Jordan. Gloria would often join her grandmother when she went to work at the Landis home, and Lois enjoyed having a playmate. The big silent house became less lonely now that Lois had someone to play outdoors with. At the time, it was unusual for children of different races to develop relationships and become friends.[19] The fact that Gloria was black and from the "colored section" of town, while Lois was white and lived in a huge house, did not seem to bother the girls.

Summer days were spent playing hopscotch and roller-skating along the brick sidewalks of their quiet neighborhood. Lois and her family also spent time at her grandparents' summer lake home. The property had an old stone blacksmith shop on it, and Lois and her friends were warned not to play there because of rattlesnakes. But they did anyway. They tested themselves by walking close to the abandoned building only to run away shrieking with panic and delight when they imagined they heard the rattle of a snake.[20]

> **[In] her secret staircase, she could go anywhere.**

In the wintertime, Gloria and Lois played in the snow, leaving twin sets of footprints behind them.[21] Years later, Lois found herself deeply saddened when she received awful news. Like the footprints they had once made together, Gloria vanished during her freshman year of college. Gloria had been murdered. This tragic event wedged itself into Lois's memory and many years would go by before she tapped into it.

Lois began school in Carlisle and attended Franklin School. It was close enough for her to walk to. In the first grade, Lois was bored with the books in the classroom. Her reading skills were far above the simple Dick and Jane books that her classmates read. Her teachers took notice and moved her into third grade where the reading was more challenging.[22]

From this point on, Lois was always the youngest and sometimes smallest in her class. Reading came with ease, but she struggled in math, specifically multiplication tables. Because she skipped a grade level, Lois lacked the knowledge in arithmetic that she should have learned in second grade.[23]

Lois's elementary school did not promote creativity the way schools do today. There was no reading of fiction (unless it was for learning purposes), no poetry, no creative writing, and no school library.[24]

By the time she was six years old, Lois was allowed to walk to the public library without an adult. She began to spend a lot of time there and sometimes returned the same day to pick out more books. The librarian limited Lois's visits by

Lois at eleven years old.

telling her that she would be allowed only one visit per day. After that, Lois began to choose thicker and harder books, much to the dismay of the librarian.[25]

When Lois was ten, she checked out *A Tree Grows in Brooklyn*, even though the librarian insisted it was inappropriate for a girl her age. Lois took it home against the librarian's wishes. She enjoyed the book so much that it ended up being one of her favorites.[26] It was around this time that Lois began to yearn in her heart to become a writer someday.

The years Lois spent in Pennsylvania were very special to her, and she would later look back on them fondly. Growing from a little girl into a young lady in the small college town of Carlisle also had its heartaches. Christmases had everything the holiday brings: decorated trees, presents, turkey and all trimmings. But there was always a hole. It was an enormous hole that could only be filled by her father, who was thousands of miles away in Japan.[27]

That hole, that empty void, would be filled with exciting news by the time Lois reached the sixth grade. Her mother was moving the family once again. This time, the move would take them to a faraway place—to Japan to join her father.[28]

Chapter 4

The Beginning of Elsewhere

It was 1948 and even though the war had ended, Lois's father was still stationed in Japan with the United States Military's occupational forces. News that her family was moving to join him meant an end to the six years that Lois had spent in Pennsylvania. She was the only sixth-grade student at Franklin School who would not be moving on to the neighborhood junior high school. Instead, Lois would be traveling across the Pacific to be reunited with her father in Tokyo.[1]

Lois's class had been studying Japan in their geography textbooks. When it was her turn to give an oral report on Japan, she casually inserted the news that an upcoming journey would soon transport her to this exotic location. She included details of eating with chopsticks, wearing wooden clogs and a flowered silk kimono.[2] With a bit of smugness, she presented her report with a subtle message: The rest of you will still be in this boring town. Sayonara![3]

With dramatic flair, eleven-year-old Lois fantasized about her farewell scene. She imagined giving a wave of her hand while narrating: "She stood on the deck of the ship, sunlight outlining her blonde hair. Below, on the dock, her classmates ached with envy . . ."[4]

Before Lois could leave the United States and move to Japan, she was required to receive a series of injections for immunization against several diseases. The inoculations for typhus, cholera, typhoid, yellow fever, and encephalitis made her miserable and sick. She spent the summer fighting the fevers that often came with these vaccinations.[5]

All the visits to doctors and painful shots were worth it though. Lois was thrilled with the idea of moving to a foreign world. At this age, she was already deep into living a writer's life. With her imagination, and the fact she was both an introvert and an observer, relocating to Japan was the most exhilarating thing to ever happen to her.

Lois's sister, Helen, did not share Lois's excitement since it meant leaving all of her ninth-grade friends behind. Little brother, Jon, was only five at this time and showed no concerns about moving.[6]

The long voyage on the ocean liner began in New York and then proceeded through the Panama Canal. Lois and her family sailed up the West

Coast to San Francisco where the ship made a stop to let more passengers aboard. After several days in San Francisco, the trip continued to the Aleutian Islands and across the Pacific to Yokohama.[7]

The first week of the month-long journey across the ocean made Lois very seasick. In those days, medicine to combat seasickness was not available, so Lois had to wait it out. She was not the only one suffering, and compared to a sailor who had to be taken off the ship by stretcher because of appendicitis, her seasickness was a bargain.[8]

When Lois's health returned, she spent the last three weeks on board trying to keep the excruciating boredom away. After all, this was not a vacation cruise. It was simply a way to get from one place to another. Since activities on the ship were limited, Lois and Helen played chess to occupy their time. Boredom also had an effect on Lois's mother so she taught Lois and Helen to play cards.[9] Playing bridge helped pass the time for all of them but it was still slow going.

Many of the passengers on the ocean liner were women and children, and Lois was able to make one close friend. Nancy was the same age as Lois, and the two of them hung out together. There was a playroom for the younger children, and Lois liked to help out in there because she enjoyed toddlers. One of the more memorable events during the trip was a costume party held for the children. Since smoking was not looked upon as a bad, unhealthy habit at the time, Lois dressed as a pack of Lucky Strike cigarettes.[10]

When the ship finally arrived in Japan, there were two very important things waiting for Lois: her father and her green bicycle. Robert Hammersberg met his family in Yokohama, and they all loaded into his car to drive to their new home. As they drove toward Tokyo, all of Lois's dreams of eating with chopsticks and wearing a kimono seemed more real. Through the car windows, she viewed Mt. Fuji and the Imperial Palace and it all seemed to be right out of the pages of a book to her.[11]

> **Mt. Fuji and the Imperial Palace . . . seemed to be right out of the pages of a book.**

At one point during the car ride, Lois's father stopped beside a run-down house. It was very shabby and dirty, with laundry hanging from the windows and hordes of people milling around. He turned to Lois's mother and said, "Welcome to our new home." Her face expressed how horrified she was, but it was a joke. Robert laughed and started the car, and they continued on their way.

For Lois, though, during those few moments when the thought of living in a slum seemed real, she was okay with it. She imagined herself living there and making changes to her life in order to manage in such a place. Her writer's imagination was at work even when faced with the possibility of hard times.[12]

The entire Hammersberg family, now complete with both parents, moved to Washington Heights— a small village that was smack-dab in the middle of Tokyo. Lois had envisioned her new home in Japan to have sliding walls and straw-matted floors, but that was not to be.[13]

Washington Heights was an American enclave. The neighborhood was built to be like a mini-United States of America and had everything a Westerner would find back home. It was sort of a replica of an American town that had been plopped down right in the center of a sprawling Japanese city. The little community was made up of American-style houses, a movie theater that showed American movies, a small church, a library, and an elementary school.[14]

Washington Heights was a safe, comfortable, American-style community filled with other military families from the United States, but there was one thing that constantly reminded Lois that she was in a very different place. The entire community was surrounded by a wall, and even though Lois was not a rebellious girl, she was a curious one.

Lois's green bike became her tool for freedom. Without her parents' knowledge, she would ride through the gate of the compound's wall and into the crowded streets of Shibuya.[15] Time after time, Lois rode down the hill that led to the neighboring

village where she could be part of the day-to-day
bustle of Japanese life.

The district of Shibuya throbbed with activity
and provided a stark contrast to the environment
Lois was accustomed to in the enclave. She ven-
tured to crowded areas where street vendors
worked and Japanese people visited shops and the-
aters. She felt safe in the streets of Shibuya and
took in all they had to offer. Smells of fish, fertil-
izer, and charcoal filled the air. Music, shouting,
and the clatter of wooden shoes, wooden sticks,
and wooden wheels filled her ears.[16]

This was a time of government turmoil and
Lois did not realize, until years later, that the loud
shouts and clatter she had heard were the sounds
of unrest. The noise came from groups of young
men who were Communist demonstrators. They
wore headbands and carried banners as they
revolted in the streets.[17]

Lois never felt that she was in danger during
her ventures out, even though sneaking away from
the safe and familiar village of Washington Heights
was daring. There was so much to see and experience that fear never crossed her mind. There were
lots of little children, and she took particular
notice of the Japanese babies and toddlers who
were dressed in bright colors of pink, orange, and
red.

Lois also noticed groups of older children who
were about her age. As she stood on the outskirts of
the Japanese school, she would watch the schoolchildren shout and play around their schoolyard.

Lois wears traditional Japanese clothes in Tokyo, 1949.

They were all dressed alike in their blue and white uniforms, and she was too shy to speak to any of them. Some of them noticed Lois and her bicycle, but they never tried to speak to her.[18] But there was one boy whose eyes met hers and the two of them stared at each other until Lois mounted her bike and rode away.[19]

In Tokyo, Lois attended Meguro School where most of the students were also military kids. She loved the academic part of school and preferred to do things on her own. She never had schoolgirl dreams of being a cheerleader, chorus member, or anything else that required her to join a club. The types of things that were required of club members just did not interest Lois. Having to learn a pledge, earn a badge, or turn a cartwheel was not high on her to-do list.

Even though she was not very interested in extracurricular activities at school, her impeccable grammar skills and nice handwriting often got her elected as class secretary. But Lois often "forgot" to take notes for the club.[20]

Away from Meguro School, there was Sunday school, which Lois skipped whenever she could. And even though she was part of a Girl Scout troop and once went along on a trip to Karuizawa, a resort town in the mountains, Lois boycotted meetings as much as possible.

There was one club that did get Lois's attention though. It was called Teenage Club, and Lois spent every Saturday night there. It was open to teenagers, but junior high students were allowed to go, too. It was a fun, social time with lots of other kids and dancing.[21]

By the time Lois was twelve, she had made many friends, and sometimes they would ride their bikes to explore parts of Tokyo. Other times, they would ride a bus or train through the city. Dressed in their American-style blue jeans and sneakers, they traveled to areas of the city that were still in distress and recovering from the war. Rubble littered the streets and some Japanese families lived in makeshift houses made from packing crates or sheets of tin.[22]

When they were not out exploring the city, Lois and her friends spent a lot of their summer at the pool. The pool was originally built to be used for the Olympics, but the games in Japan were canceled because of the war. Lois rode her bike there and swam for endless hours with all of her friends.

While she was in the seventh grade, one of Lois's best friends moved away from Washington Heights to the island of Eta Jima in southern Japan. At vacation time, Lois was invited to visit her friend. Twice she traveled by train to get there.

Just like Tokyo, the island also showed signs of war. Dangerous areas of woods were roped off to prevent anyone from entering and being killed. Signs posted with scary words—UNEXPLODED LAND MINES—warned of the danger. When they came across these signs, the twelve-year-old playmates were cautious and stayed far away.[23]

At her home in Washington Heights, there were a few changes to the life Lois had known in

America. Since it was not unusual for military families to hire help while they stayed in Tokyo, the Hammersbergs had two maids who worked for them. Ritsuko and Teruko sometimes wore their traditional Japanese kimonos for special occasions or holidays. Lois also had a beautiful kimono to wear, but shopping for everyday clothing in Tokyo was limited. Most military families did their shopping and bought their clothes at the Tokyo Post Exchange, or PX. That was fine for play and school clothes, but it meant that Lois and her friends all wore the same outfits.[24]

Outside of the PX, Lois also had the choice of having clothing made for her, but that was risky. If the seamstress did not get the pattern right, there was a chance Lois would end up wearing a dress she did not like. It was a risk she was not willing to take, since her mother probably would have made her wear any imperfect dress—even one with sausage-like sleeves.[25]

Lois was allowed to order a special dress from the Sears' catalog when she was twelve. It was red plaid with a delicate lace trim on the bottom, and she planned to wear it for Christmas. It took several weeks for the dress to arrive, and it fit her fine. Her father took a photograph of Lois standing with Ritsuko and Teruko, but in the picture, there was something missing. Sound! Lois loved the dress but did not realize that the fabric was so noisy. The taffeta made a swishing sound every time she moved, and she hated that.[26]

Many holidays and birthdays came and went

during her stay in Japan, but one of the biggest milestones in any girl's life was reached while she was there. She became a full-fledged teenager and celebrated her thirteenth birthday in Tokyo. This was a very special birthday for Lois because she was now a teen and because her father remembered her day with a very special gift. Her gave her a Smith Corona typewriter with dark green keys and her name engraved on the case.[27]

Lois's father purchased the typewriter at the Tokyo PX, and it was an incredible gift to receive in 1950. It meant a lot to Lois, especially because she had begun to view her family as two sets of matched pairs. One set was her sister and mother, who were quite domestic and organized and shared an interest in sewing. The other set was her brother and father, who did boy-related things like playing with electric trains or chemistry sets. Lois did not have any interest in domestics or boy things, so when she received the Smith Corona, she felt that her father understood her and her future dreams.[28]

The summer after Lois's birthday, the Korean War began and Japan became an unsafe place to live. Lois was uprooted once again in 1950 when all American women and children were forced to evacuate. Lois's mother had no choice but to take the children back to Pennsylvania.[29] Lois's father stayed behind, but this time their separation did not last long. Once he was back on American soil and reunited with the family, the Hammersberg family moved to New York and lived at an Army base on Governors Island.

Lois enjoyed living at the new Army base and having other kids from military families around her. Growing up as a child of a military officer, Lois was comfortable around other "Army brats" and never felt pressured to fit in as a new kid. There was a certain amount of camaraderie and understanding between teenagers who had spent their lives moving from Army post to Army post.[30]

When it came time to start her freshman year at Curtis High School in Staten Island, New York, Lois did have a hard time trying to fit in. She was still a shy student who loved to read and write, and now she found herself in a large school where she did not know a soul. She ended up transferring in and out of several other schools before finally finding a smaller school that fit her needs. Packer Collegiate Institute was a private school for girls in Brooklyn Heights, New York, and as usual, Lois loved English classes but still detested gym class.[31]

When Lois graduated from Packer Collegiate Institute in 1954, a caption underneath her yearbook photograph predicted what she might become. It read: "future novelist," and it was a testimony to the impression she had made on her classmates and teachers.[32]

Lois's dream of becoming a novelist got even closer when she was awarded a scholarship to attend Pembroke College in Providence, Rhode Island. Armed with her writing skills and Smith Corona typewriter, Lois was on her way to make her dream a reality.

Lois's senior high school portrait, age seventeen.

Chapter 5

Love, Grief, and Making Trades

Lois was seventeen when she became a college freshman in the fall of 1954. Pembroke College was the women's branch of Brown University, and it was full of young women who all seemed to wear stylish cashmere sweaters and dirty sneakers. Lois lived in one of the dormitories, and it did not take long for her begin socializing with her college classmates.[1]

Lois had once described her thirteen-year-old self as "an odd loner of an adolescent, secretive and privately dramatic,"[2] but it seems college helped her blossom into a more outgoing person. The dorm she lived in was a private home that had been converted to house college students. Lois shared the house with fourteen other girls.

When she was not studying or working hard in

the honors program for aspiring writers, she did what most teenage girls did during the fifties. They played the card game bridge, and twisted their hair into pin curls in order to get the curly locks that were all the rage at the time. But mostly, Lois and her friends waited for the phone to ring.[3]

The dorm rooms were often filled with a smoky haze because some of the college girls puffed on cigarettes while they played cards or knitted. They kept themselves busy until the phone rang. And when it did, Lois and her dorm mates would freeze until they found out who it was that had a date. Having a date lined up for Saturday night was not only important, it was essential.[4]

Young men and dating were a big part of Lois's college days, and she was fitting in more and more. Wearing her plaid wool skirts, knee socks and loafers, Lois was now a part of a group of girls who were a lot alike. Besides boys and fashion, the classmates also had something else in common: *brains*. The girls in Lois's dorm came from all over the United States, and some had been class presidents or valedictorians at their high schools. They were the cream of the crop and good grades were easy to come by, even in college.[5]

Lois excelled during her freshman year and was awarded with A's for her writing. In her sophomore year, she majored in English expression, which was a fancy term for "writing."[6] At the time, most of Lois's stories were sweet, sad stories. Sometimes, they were about small children and dying dogs.[7]

In the special honors program, Lois had a

professor assigned to her as a mentor. She was required to meet with him to discuss her writing, and he offered her encouragement. During one of their meetings, the beefy professor with the pink face told Lois something that she already knew— that her grammar was impeccable and her writing was fluent.[8]

Even though the professor was complimenting Lois, she got the feeling that her good grammar and ability to make words flow was not enough for him. He puffed on his pipe as Lois waited for him to offer her guidance. And then, finally, after staring at her with mournful, bloodshot eyes, he suggested that Lois had not experienced much yet.[9]

"Like what?" Lois asked him, thinking she had experienced quite a lot in her eighteen years. But when the professor explained that she had not yet dealt with major life lessons, such as grief, Lois had to agree.[10] The professor was probably trying to tell Lois that her writing would become stronger once she felt deep emotion. Even though it was true, Lois privately hoped she would never have to deal with grief.

Lois was able to relax a little when their mentoring session took a turn and they began to talk about love. The professor suggested that love was a similar experience to grief. He might have been trying to say that both of the emotions bring on yearning, wishing, and aching since they both involve the heart. Lois left the meeting and headed back to the dorm with her writing in hand.

Grief had not been something she had experienced yet, but love was a different story. Love was something she could relate to. Love was *her* department.[11]

Lois had fallen for a college senior during her sophomore year at Pembroke. Donald Grey Lowry had joined the United States Navy and already had plans to move to California, and he wanted Lois to move with him. He asked Lois to marry him, and she was willing to make a trade. She was ready for a change of scenery, adventure, and romance—and freedom from college rules.[12]

> **Grief had not been something she had experienced yet, but love was a different story.**

To make the trade, though, Lois had to give up something in return. She decided that love and marriage were more important to her than a college education. So she sacrificed the degree she was working toward. She had loved writing papers and loved doing research, but now there was one thing she loved more than those things and it was becoming Mrs. Donald Lowry.[13]

Around this same time, Lois received a letter from a law firm in Philadelphia. The document stated that she was named in the estate of Edward MacFunn Biddle III. At first, Lois did not recognize the name of the man who had left her money after his death. As she read the letter further, it explained that Biddle was leaving money to the little girl in pink pajamas who had recited poetry in her grandfather's parlor in 1942.[14] Lowry then remembered Biddle to be someone very special from her past.

Lois now had a large check, a diamond engagement ring, and a new outlook on her future. In June 1956, Donald and Lois became husband and wife and packed up their light blue Pontiac and headed for California. They drove to San Diego with their car filled with wedding gifts and stacks of books that Lois would not leave behind. She may have traded college for marriage, but there was one thing she did not trade. She kept her passion for literature and language and one other important tool—her Smith Corona typewriter.

At nineteen years old, Lowry was a military wife living in a small apartment in Pacific Beach. Since Donald Lowry was off on a six-month Navy cruise to the Far East, Lois got a job as a receptionist in a doctor's office. Being a lover of both dogs and books, she bought a dog to keep her company and got herself a library card.[15]

As a military wife, Lowry spent several years moving from one location to another with her husband. After California came Connecticut, the birthplace of their first daughter, Alix, who was born in 1958. Lowry gave birth to their son Grey while they were living in Florida in 1959, but that stay did not last long either. The family moved on to Charleston, South Carolina, for a year before

Lois Lowry in her wedding gown in 1956.

moving yet again to Cambridge, Massachusetts, where Donald entered Harvard Law School.[16]

With her husband out of the military and studying law, Lowry took on part-time work to help pay the bills for their growing family.[17] When she was not working out of the house, she was busy taking care of the house and children, and there was not much time for writing anymore. She had become a domesticated 1950s mother, but her childhood dream of being a writer had not completely disappeared. It was simply put on hold for a while and stored away in a closet along with the Smith Corona.

While still living in Massachusetts in 1961, Lowry had another daughter, Kristin. She was now a full-time mother and homemaker and spent a lot of time telling stories and reading to her young-sters. Not long after Kristin came along, Lowry became pregnant with her fourth child.

In the fall of 1962, the Lowry family lived in a less-than-perfect two-bedroom apartment and struggled with money. Even though they were quite poor, Lowry returned to school to take a course in creative writing. She was thrilled to be writing again. Taking the course helped her regain her childhood love of words and sentences and placing them on a page.[18]

Taking care of three young children while she was seven months pregnant, Lowry struggled to find time to write her assignments. She made time early in the mornings before her children woke up, and it was a joy to play with words again. She juggled her homework assignments between laundry, cooking, strolling to the playground, and reading bedtime stories.[19]

Lowry's renewed interest in writing and the joy of expecting a new baby were dampened with sad news. Lowry learned that her sister, Helen, had been diagnosed with cancer and did not have long to live. This was a time of many emotions, and it would not be long before Lowry would experience what she had privately wished she never would: Grief.

In her pregnant state, Lowry was not able to travel to visit Helen. She stayed home and cared for her children and continued to go to her writing class. In November 1962, Lowry missed one class because of a very important event: Benjamin Lowry was born.[20]

When Lowry returned to class the following week, her enthusiasm for the course was ruined when her professor made a rude comment to her. "Glad to see you've done *something* creative this semester!" he told her sarcastically. She felt deflated and chose not to return to the class again.

Lowry was a busy mother and happy raising her children. But having four little ones under the age of five and attending school was too much. She realized that her interest in taking classes would have to wait. The timing was wrong. She decided to make another trade in her life. She traded creative writing for motherhood.

About a month after Lowry gave birth to Benjamin, she received the heartbreaking news that

Helen had passed away. Lowry was twenty-five and full of grief and sadness about the loss of her sister. As much as she had wanted to, Lowry had never been able to make the trip to see Helen while she was still alive.[21] Instead, she made the trip back to Pennsylvania to attend Helen's funeral. The death affected Lowry deeply, and as she stood in front of the funeral home with her brother, Jon, she became aware and frightened about how easily everything could all slip away.[22]

In 1963, the Lowry family moved from their apartment in Cambridge, Massachusetts, to a farmhouse in Portland, Maine. The home had lots and lots of books, and there was always a dog or cat curled in a sunny spot somewhere. They even had a barn where they kept their horse. Recalling these early years, Lowry once said she could "change a diaper with one hand, write a magazine article with the other and stir spaghetti sauce in between."[23]

Lowry has also been known to say, "My children grew up in Maine, and so did I." She did all the things most mothers did, like joining committees and attending Tupperware parties, but she also went back to college. When her youngest child began school in 1968, Lowry enrolled in the University of Southern Maine to work toward her degree. At thirty-one, she was doing homework alongside her children as they sat around the big pine table that had once belonged to her grandmother.[24]

Soon, Lowry needed a kid-free space where she

could work alone. She took over one of the rooms in the family's farmhouse and set her typewriter up in there. This was the one part of the house that Lois declared off-limits to the kids and dogs. Other than that, Lowry was not a strict rule maker.

Her blue-eyed children were energetic, bright, and fun loving. On top of that, they were readers. Twenty-five years after Lowry had read *A Tree Grows in Brooklyn*, her daughters curled up with it. Lowry did not take chores too seriously even though she nagged sometimes. She did not really mind when the kids did not clean their rooms.[25]

Along with studying literature in college, Lowry also took photography classes and set up a darkroom in her basement. She had signed up for the

> **"My children grew up in Maine, and so did I."**
>
> **—Lois Lowry**

classes as a way to earn college credits, but it did not take long for her to become fascinated by the art of it. For Lowry, photography and writing were closely related because both involved capturing a subject in just the right way.[26]

After Lowry graduated from college in 1972, she was working toward her master's degree when an opportunity arose. A friend who had worked for a publisher hired her to write two books for

J. Westson Walch, a textbook publisher. Lowry was finally able to do what she had wanted to do since childhood—write professionally. There was an added bonus in writing the books, too. All the work and research she put into the textbooks qualified as independent studies and went toward her degree.[27]

Lowry's first book, *Black American Literature*, was published in 1973, and her second book, *Literature of the American Revolution*, was published in 1974. With the experience of writing the textbooks, Lowry became more interested in writing and photography than school. She dropped out of her master's program to pursue her writing career and wrote several articles for *The New York Times*.

One of those articles was a very funny account about her appearance on the television show *Jeopardy!* In the 1974 article, "How Does It Feel To Be on a TV Quiz Show? Don't Ask," Lowry broke down the behind-the-scenes making of the program as well as the show itself. She wrote about having her makeup done by a *Jeopardy!* crew member and how that person darkened only one of her eyebrows. This gave her a quizzical appearance as she tried to keep pace with the other contestants.

While Lowry competed and answered several questions right, she also experienced some technical difficulties. She recounted them humorously by writing: "A peculiar paralysis sets in, affecting only my right index finger, and question after question, to which I know the answer, goes by without my pushing the button."

Lowry's writing style shone in her freelance work, and she found more success when her story, "Crow Call," was purchased by *Redbook Magazine* in 1975.

This was Lowry's first piece of fiction to get published. She drew upon her childhood memories for inspiration and created a story that sold. After several more sales of fiction pieces, Lowry really started to find success with her writing. At the same time, she also was finding herself a bit more. At thirty-nine years old, she was working as a freelance journalist and photographer and, because her kids were older now, she was able to go out on assignments more often.

It was around this time that Melanie Kroupa, the editor at Houghton Mifflin Publishers, wrote to Lowry about writing books for children. Kroupa was a young editor who was actively looking for new authors, and she saw something special in the way Lowry used descriptions to capture the emotions of the characters in her story "Crow Call."[28] Lowry had been turning stories from her past into fictionalized retellings for some time, and she liked to reminisce about her childhood, so the idea of writing for children appealed to her. She was actually surprised it had not occurred to her before.[29]

Using the same Smith Corona she had received from her father when she was thirteen years old, Lowry dove into writing her first book for children, *A Summer to Die*. As a young girl, spending endless hours scribbling stories and poems in notebooks, Lowry probably did not ever dream that she would grow up to write about grief and the death of a sister. But at thirty-nine, Lowry was now able to use the emotion that her former college professor had told her she needed to experience. *A Summer to Die* was a story loosely based on her own life experiences and emotions. When it was complete, it was time for Lowry to send it off to the editor.

When Melanie Kroupa received the manuscript, it was originally titled *A Season to Flower, A Summer to Die*. Kroupa was supposed to leave for vacation, but instead she closed her office door and read the story in one sitting. The ending made her cry, and she ran out of her office and shouted, "We have to publish this!"

About the same time that Lowry was beginning to find success as a newly discovered author, her marriage of twenty-one years was ending in divorce. Her career as an author of children's books officially began when Houghton Mifflin Publishers bought *A Summer to Die* and published it in 1977. This first book paved the way for Lowry's journey to success, but it was a journey she would now be traveling alone.

Chapter 6

Journeys of the Heart

After years of living on the sprawling farm where she raised her family, Lowry packed only the basic necessities into her little Honda Civic and moved away. She found an apartment over a garage, and since it was already furnished, it was easy for Lowry to settle in. She simply unpacked her clothes and her typewriter. Then, an important new addition to her meager belongings came in the form of a gift from one of her biggest fans. Her father sent her an electric typewriter to celebrate the publication of her first book.[1]

Not having a lot of stuff was a good thing for Lowry. It made her realize what was really important to her. Four of the most important things to her were her children, and even though they did not live in the garage apartment with her, they did visit. Her two oldest kids were in college and the two younger kids were still in high school. They spent time at both parents' homes.

After spending the summer living in the garage apartment, Lowry found a house to rent for the winter. Having more space meant her kids were able to live with her. Her daughter Kristin moved in with her and Ben, her youngest son, came on weekends. The two oldest kids were off at college and had started their own lives by this point.

Lowry had money struggles, but she was able to pay her rent and buy food for herself. In the few times she had any money left over, she bought books. As her collection grew, she made herself some bookcases with simple planks of wood.[2]

In order to support herself, Lowry learned to be very self-disciplined. She got in the habit of going to work at her typewriter every morning.[3] During the months she lived in her Maine apartment, Lowry wrote her second book, *Find a Stranger, Say Goodbye*.[4] By this time, she had formed a solid relationship with the staff at Houghton Mifflin and was working with the head of the children's department, editor Walter Lorraine.

Lowry had received a few fan letters after *A Summer to Die* began selling well, and she enjoyed hearing from her readers. The book was also receiving good reviews. But, being so new in the book business, Lowry did not fully understand what "doing well" meant when it came to book sales or reviews. When Walter Lorraine called Lowry to tell her that *A Summer to Die* was getting starred reviews, he kindly explained to her what that meant.[5]

Plainly put, a starred review in any publication was a sign that the reviewers felt the book was outstanding compared to other books they had read. After reading *A Summer to Die*, a reviewer for *School Library Journal* wrote: "Lowry is skillful both in evoking a sense of place and in depicting realistic and sympathetic characters. Her story captures the mysteries of living and dying without manipulating the readers' emotions, providing understanding and a comforting sense of completion."[6]

Lois Lowry with her four children in 1993.

Lowry's writing has such a true-to-life quality because of her ability to pluck detailed memories and emotions from her past. Readers relate to the events and characters she portrays in her books because she recreates people she has known and things she has experienced. Once readers know her life story, it becomes clear what parts of her books may have come directly from her own childhood and adult life.

In *A Summer to Die*, the characters Meg and Molly are sisters whose relationship closely resembles the one shared between Lowry and her sister, Helen. Lowry was twenty-five at the time she lost her sister to cancer, and in the book, Meg is thirteen when Molly dies. Lowry's own personal experience of losing her sister had to have an impact when she created the characters and put them in the story that was much like her own.

Even though Lowry drew from her own knowledge of what it is like to lose a sister, *A Summer to Die* is not autobiographical. But there are segments peppered throughout her story that savvy readers may identify as having come from Lowry's life.

In one scene in *A Summer to Die*, Meg describes the differences between her old house and her new house by saying: "The difference is that the house in town was big, with a million closets and stairways and windows and an attic, all sorts of places for privacy and escape: places where you could curl up with a book and no one would know you were there for hours."[7] Perhaps as Lowry wrote this, she was back in that hidden staircase at her grandparents' house and using that memory to give her character personality.

Lowry had once said that "*A Summer to Die* wrenched open the excruciating door of loss."[8] The fact that Lowry used events and emotions from her past and remixed them to create realistic fiction is what made her writing so engaging. Young readers and reviewers were not the only ones who saw something very special in *A Summer to Die*. In 1978, the International Reading Association (IRA) honored *A Summer to Die* by naming it the year's winner of the Children's Book Award.

"*A Summer to Die* wrenched open the excruciating door of loss."

—Lois Lowry

It was a spring day when Lowry answered a phone call from the president of the International Reading Association and received the news. Once again, Lowry was unsure of what this meant, so she contacted her editor for guidance. When she told Lorraine that the IRA wanted her to go to their national convention in Houston, Texas, to receive her award, she was embarrassed because she could not afford to go.[9] So when Lorraine informed her that Houghton Mifflin would send her there, Lowry was probably relieved.

Walter Lorraine attended the award banquet with Lowry, his newly published author, and as they sat in a room filled with two thousand people, Lowry asked him, "Do I have to make a speech?" His face whitened as he responded, "You mean you don't have a speech?"[10]

Lorraine worried about Lowry's ability to handle the pressure of giving her acceptance speech. His palms got sweaty as he offered her advice and hints on what she should say to her live audience. He was trying to reassure Lowry before she went up to accept her award, but Lowry was confident and patted her editor's hand and said, "There, there, don't worry, everything will turn out all right."[11] And it did. That day, Lowry gave her first public speech, while the editor who would go on to publish all of her future books sat and listened. It must have been a very proud moment for both of them.

Lowry's second book, *Find a Stranger, Say Goodbye*, had already been published when she began working on *Autumn Street*. But when the winter of 1979 rolled around, Lowry set aside *Autumn Street* and traded it for a book that had a much lighter tone. *Anastasia Krupnik* was a book that made Lowry laugh during the cold and snowy days in Maine.[12]

Switching gears to create freckle-faced, ten-year-old Anastasia Krupnik was a very good decision for Lowry. The book was published in 1979 and quickly became a popular title. Readers fell in love with Anastasia and the Krupnik family and the funny story Lowry told. The year it was published, it was named an American Library Association Notable Book.[13]

Up to this point, Lowry's books dealt with more serious themes, so writing humorous books had to be a welcome change for her. After admitting that she had been a painfully introverted child herself, Lowry once said, "I would have loved to be a wise-cracking blabbermouth like Anastasia."[14]

Having daughters of her own helped inspire Lowry when she was writing funny stories. Talking about the character she created, Lowry said, "She's probably a mixture of my two quite nutty daughters."[15] *Anastasia Krupnik* was the first book in what would become a very successful series for Lowry. Ideas for each book came in various ways, and since she had her girls as good sources for comic behavior, all Lowry needed to do was think of a new plot or a new problem for Anastasia to overcome.

From 1979 to 1995, Lowry threw Anastasia and her family into many funny situations and wrote nine books for the series. Walter Lorraine described the series perfectly when he wrote, "The Anastasia stories are very funny, but woven into that humor is far more worldly insight than is usual for such popular fiction."[16]

After the first *Anastasia* book was published, Lowry continued to juggle her writing between freelance assignments and books. In the summer of 1979, a magazine Lowry was writing for sent her to an island off the coast of Maine to cover a story about Carl Nelson, a painter who lived there all alone.[17]

As Lowry photographed and interviewed Nelson, it became clear to her that he had an ability to see color in a way that she did not. Because of her background in photography, Lowry knew that she had a pretty good visual sense, but as she listened to Nelson, she realized that the ability he possessed to see color went way beyond hers. She was grateful that their talk about colors, perspective, and composition enabled her to see things differently.[18]

> **For Lowry, writing and photography were closely related.**

For Lowry, writing and photography were closely related. It was important for her to see things from various points of views and angles. Meeting Carl Nelson helped her do that. This may have been one of the reasons that Lowry ended up keeping one of the photographs she had taken of him. The picture of him, with his long graying beard and deep wrinkles, showed a man with a thoughtful expression. There was something about his eyes and his face that haunted Lowry. She hung the photograph above her desk and thought of Nelson often. Years went by before Lowry heard the news that the man who once had such a gift for seeing color had gone blind.[19]

Before 1979 was through, Lowry made two important decisions that changed the course of her life forever. At a time when she was deciding what to do with her life, Lowry chose to give up free-lance journalism in order to concentrate on writing for children.[20]

Even though Lowry had loved Maine, the long, cold winters there had become lonely. The small village on the sea was beautiful, but it was not a very convenient place to live. In order to see a movie—something Lowry really enjoyed doing—she had to drive twenty minutes into town. During Maine's heavy snowstorms, even her mailman could not get through at times. Lowry ended her isolation and moved to Boston, Massachusetts, after living in Maine for sixteen years.[21]

Lowry seemed to have it all: a career as a ris-ing author, great kids, and a new home. Her new environment gave her a change of scenery, but there was still something missing. Then, at forty-two, Lowry entered the dating scene and found her soul mate.

Chapter 7

Push a Button

After her divorce in 1977, Lowry went on several dates over a two-year period but they turned out to be disappointing. As a woman in her forties, Lowry found dating was just not the same as it had been when she was a teenager. At any age, finding the right dress and having normal conversations is all part of the dating scene. But, at forty, most of Lowry's dates were less than perfect. After being paired up with men who wanted to borrow money from her, or wanted her to join strange religions, or even worse yet, were still married, Lowry decided dating was not her thing. She was not interested in dating anymore and joked that she would become a hermit instead. Then one day, a gentleman named Martin Small called her up and asked her out for coffee.[1]

Lowry knew Small casually because she was a customer of the insurance agency where he worked. So even though she had given up on the whole dating scene, Lowry agreed to meet Small. During their date, Small made an odd comment to one of Lowry's suggestions. He said, "You have good ideas, Cornelius. When I am king I will give you a green hat." Lowry sat there in her bluish-green dress thinking, *Oh, great. I am having a cup of coffee with a weirdo*. But, thankfully, Small went on to explain that he was quoting a line from the popular children's book *Babar*.[2]

Lowry realized that a man who recited lines from children's books was probably a pretty good guy. In addition to the fact that they were both divorced with four children, they also shared a love for classical music. Finding they had several things in common, Lowry and Small hit it off and began to see one another on a regular basis. Lowry's life as a hermit did not last long. In 1980, the couple began a new life together in an area of Boston called Beacon Hill. This was the same year that a novel Lowry had once set aside was published.

Autumn Street was another novel Lowry wrote using real events from her past. Many authors use their past to get story ideas, but Lowry's ability to use her memory to create fiction from her experiences is exceptional. She has said that bringing childhood memories to the surface is like pushing a button. In order to go back to the days when she

Martin Small and Lois Lowry in 1992.

was five, or eight, or any other age, she can just push a button in her mind.[3]

It must have taken a lot of courage to push that button when Lowry was writing *Autumn Street*. The story of *Autumn Street* was inspired by actual events in Lowry's past that dealt with issues of injustice, prejudice, and loss.[4]

Even though Lowry changed the events to fit the story line, the characters in *Autumn Street* were based on real people from Lowry's childhood. For the book, Lowry used her childhood self for the role of the main character, Elizabeth Lorimer. She cast a character named Charles to recreate her real childhood friend, Gloria Jordan.[5] And Fleta Jordan, the beloved woman from Lowry's past, played the part of Tatie, the housekeeper.

The events in *Autumn Street* mirrored much of Lowry's real life, and she did not sugarcoat the awful parts when she wrote the story. In the book, the murder of fictional Charles reflects the unfortunate death of Gloria Jordan. Gloria was actually killed after the girls had grown up and gone off to college,[6] but the characters in *Autumn Street* are much younger. Lowry's relationship with Gloria's grandmother, Fleta, was also portrayed in the book.

Because *Autumn Street* dealt with many dark issues, Lowry's publisher struggled with marketing the book. There was uncertainty about whether the book was geared toward adults or children.[7] The decision was made to publish it as a book for children, but when *The New Yorker* reviewed it, it was not listed as a children's book.[8] Other reviewers did classify it in the children's category, however, and it went on to receive starred reviews.

Lowry has become known as the author who writes about the connections people make with each other. Human relationships have always been important to her. She has said, "No matter how uneventful a life may seem, there are many moments of enhanced emotions that do lend themselves to fiction."[9]

Lowry's skill at weaving real events into her fiction is seen in her more serious books as well as her lighter, funnier books. She has said that her fictional characters appear in her imagination as full-blown people, and she can see and hear their voices.[10] One of those voices was her Anastasia character, and it seemed she had a lot to say.

In 1981 and 1982, *Anastasia Again!* and *Anastasia at Your Service* were published and fans were delighted. Writing about Anastasia seemed to come easily for Lowry. To keep her lovable character going, all she had to do was come up with new ideas for stories. Plus, using incidents from her own kids' lives was a perfect way to give Anastasia a personality that leapt off the page.

Fans have often asked Lowry how she gets her ideas, and she has said, ". . . it's tough to explain to a kid how an idea pops into your imagination."[11] She finds ideas everywhere, all the time. The way a stranger walks or small snippets of overheard conversations are examples of things from which Lowry may get an idea. She has always been observant to what is going on around her.

Before she writes her books, Lowry spends a lot of time thinking about her ideas first. Once the story is clear in her mind, it only takes her about six months to write a book. She has never used notes or an outline and has admitted that her process is a little haphazard.[12] Hard work, fun, and a lot of waiting for the right words to come go into the writing process, and Lowry has said there is nothing magical about it.

The magic comes later for Lowry, once her part is done and her books are in the hands of her fans. Lowry has explained it like this: ". . . there is that magical somebody known as the reader. And that I have a relationship with—and an obligation to—the reader, because I affect that person's life and thinking, and that is no small responsibility."[13]

Between 1983 and 1987, Lowry produced a whopping number of books. When she added four more Anastasia books, her career as a prolific series writer was cemented in the publishing world. Her abundant success also included five more novels: *Taking Care of Terrific*, *The One Hundredth Thing About Caroline*, *Us and Uncle Fraud*, *Switcharound*, and *Rabble Starkey*.

Her next book was basically the brainchild of Lowry's faithful readers. Letters poured in from fans asking her for more information about Anastasia's little brother, Sam. But Lowry was not sold that her audience really wanted to read about a three year old. But then, his story took shape in her mind, and Sam's story was born.[14]

As if having one funny character for readers to follow was not enough, *All About Sam* was the first book in yet another series for Lowry. Sam's debut was in 1988 and he was a hoot! Lowry began his story with this laugh-out-loud scene:

> "Does he wet his diapers a whole lot?" the girl asked the man and the woman.
> Yes, he thought, I do. As a matter of fact I am wetting them right now, right at this very moment.

Once she got on a roll, it seems it was easy for Lowry to get into the head of a three year old, and readers loved it.

> ## Lowry's books ranged from serious to funny, showing her versatility as a writer.

Up to this point, the tone of Lowry's books ranged from serious to funny, showing her versatility as a writer. To get her writing juices flowing, she begins her day by reading poetry before she moves on to her own work. Lowry forms her books by placing her characters in settings that fit each story. Many of the settings she has used are places Lowry actually lived in or traveled to.

Even though Lowry used her own experiences and memories when she created her books, it was the memories of a friend that led to her novel *Number the Stars*. Lowry's friend had told her about the history of the Nazi occupation during the years she had lived in Denmark. The true stories about living in fear during a dangerous time were so remarkable to Lowry that she decided to write a novel about it.[15]

Even though *Number the Stars* was a fictional account of historical events, Lowry made sure her details were accurate. In a letter she wrote to her editor, she pointed out a couple of changes she made:

> Tough to soften the Nazis but I have them simply dropping the photos on the floor now—no crumpling or tearing. I tried to differentiate a little between the run-of-the-mill soldiers on the street and on the train, who were often confused and awkward boys, and the Gestapo types who would have been the ones to make arrests. I still have them slapping Mom, I'm afraid. Historically, they did do such things.[16]

Lowry originally titled the book *Number the Stars, One by One*, but it was changed to *Number the Stars* before it was released in 1989. Multi-talented Lowry even took the photograph that appears on *Number the Stars*. All of Lowry's research efforts and hard work paid off when book reviewers gave her novel glowing starred reviews. A reviewer for *School Library Journal* described the novel and its main character, Annemarie, by writing:

> A moving and satisfying story of heroism in war time which is totally accessible to young readers.

> Annemarie's life in occupied Copenhagen in 1943 seemingly is not much changed by the war—until the Nazi persecution of Danish Jews begins . . . *Number the Stars* brings the war to a child's level of understanding, suggesting but not detailing its horrors. It is well plotted, and period and place are convincingly recreated.[17]

Lowry's eye for detail made her characters and story come alive. Accurate facts were important to her, no matter how small they seemed. In an early draft of *Number the Stars*, Lowry had an apple pie in a scene but that changed once she became aware that using an apple pie was not historically accurate. After a friend pointed out that apple pie was an American invention, Lowry realized Danish people would have never heard of it. She ended up changing the scene to include applesauce[18] instead, and it was small facts like this that helped to make *Number the Stars* appealing to readers all over the world.

In 1990, Lowry was rewarded with the highest honor in children's literature when *Number the Stars* was given the Newbery Medal. The Newbery Medal is given out each year by the American Library Association and it is inscribed: "For the Most Distinguished Contribution to American Literature for Children." When choosing the winner, a committee looks for quality and excellence in the book that they honor with the prestigious award. *Number the Stars* certainly has both, and in the years following its release, it has sold millions of copies and has been translated into at least twenty languages.[19]

Chapter 8

Full Circle

The same year Lowry was awarded the Newbery Medal for *Number the Stars*, readers were given another glimpse into the world of the Tates. Lowry first introduced her readers to the Tate family in 1983 in *The One Hundredth Thing About Caroline* and again in 1985 in *Switcharound*. The next installment of the Tates, *Your Move, J.P.!* was released in 1990 as Lowry continued to work on her other series.

Lowry delighted her fans with additions to her Anastasia Krupnik and Sam series. *Anastasia at This Address* and *Attaboy, Sam!* were published back to back in 1991 and 1992. *Attaboy, Sam!* marked Lowry's twentieth book in fifteen years of writing.

During this time of continued success in her

professional life, Lowry was going through a difficult time in her personal life. Her parents were aging and both were very frail. Lowry often traveled to visit them at a nursing home in Virginia where they lived near her brother, Jon. Even though her mom and dad lived in the same nursing home, they lived in different sections and Lowry usually visited her mother first.[1]

Her mother's physical condition was failing but her mind, along with her memory, was still clear. She was still able to recollect all sorts of stories from her past, and Lowry often sat with her and listened. Lowry felt her mother *needed* to share her memories, and Lowry was more than willing to take them in. Her mother was very fragile, blind, and bedridden, but she had the strength to reminisce about her life. She told Lowry small incidents of her childhood as well as recounting her college years. She passed many memories on to Lowry and also spoke of the most heartbreaking day of her life: the day her daughter Helen died.[2]

Lowry's father's condition was much different from her mother's. Her father was more physically able and used a cane to slowly get around. He teased his nurses, and he remembered Lowry when she visited. But the rest of his memory was sketchy. He could not remember his own childhood, his career, or things he had enjoyed. He also did not remember his daughter Helen or what happened to her. Lowry showed him a photograph of her to help jog his memory but it was not much help. "And you say she died? How did that happen?" he asked as he frowned at the photograph.[3]

Lowry began to think about her parents' health and how they were so different. Her writer's mind shifted into gear and she began to ask herself "what if" questions. "What if there were medications, maybe a shot, they could give Dad, and he would remember Helen?" But then she also thought how sad that would be for her dad. "Why make him remember that day?"

Lowry's imagination was churning as her thoughts turned to her mom. "What if there were a shot to give Mother?" She thought about a type of shot that would allow her mom to keep all her joyous memories and only erase the painful ones, like the death of her daughter.[4]

The same year Lowry's mother died, she began to write what would become one of her most celebrated and controversial books. Once again, the main character appeared in her mind, and he began to take form. She knew his name was Jonas. And, like many of her other books, the story brewed in her imagination even though its title would not come until later. Lowry has said that coming up with titles is very tough for her and she never titles a book until it is finished.[5]

In a speech Lowry gave at the Chicago Public Library, she explained her process by saying, "I always go about the creation of a character, first. Then I set a series of events in motion—starting, usually, with one precipitating incident."[6] So with

Jonas created, Lowry threw him into an invented world and began the book with the words:

> It was almost December, and Jonas was beginning to be frightened.

This opening sentence was very familiar to Lowry. When she was a child living in Tokyo during the war, she had listened to a conversation between her parents. They spoke about moving the children back to United States because the area around their home in Tokyo was becoming unsafe. Lowry was thirteen and beginning to be scared.[7]

As she often did, Lowry turned to her own emotions and memories to write Jonas's story. But there was something else from which she drew inspiration. All those "what if" questions she had asked herself during her visits with her parents inspired her too. She set Jonas's story in the future and placed him in a community where all the people exist without memories or knowledge of the past.[8] There is no emotion, pain, crime, pleasure, or color in Jonas's controlled community.

In this seemingly perfect world, Lowry created another character and named him The Giver. The Giver, alone, holds all the memories of the past until Jonas is selected as the Receiver of Memory. Jonas and The Giver begin the task of transferring memories and as Jonas learns about the past, he begins to see his world differently and wonder about Elsewhere.

Speaking about her characters and their journeys, Lowry has said, ". . . it is only after a series of controlled surprises that a story finds its way to an ending—and only then that I can understand it, assess it, find its meaning, and create its title."[9] Lowry fittingly titled her new book *The Giver*, and it was published in 1993.

The experience of being a scared child in Tokyo and the thoughts about her parents' health helped Lowry create *The Giver*. But Carl Nelson, the painter whom Lowry interviewed in 1979, also played a part. In the last five years of his life, Nelson was blind. This was the man who helped Lowry see color in a way that she had not seen before.

Speaking about Nelson's loss of sight, Lowry has said, "That element also went into the writing of *The Giver* in a subconscious way—the fact that he went blind—lost it all, after all he had given the world." And, reflecting about the time she spent with Nelson, Lowry stated, "That aspect of someone giving me color went into the writing of the book."[10]

> **"[Blindness] also went into the writing of *The Giver*."**
>
> **—Lois Lowry**

In the novel, there is a scene between Jonas and The Giver where they realize that Jonas is beginning to see color—something that no longer exists in their community. Jonas does not know what it is, and it comes and goes in flashes and it is always the same color, red. The Giver explains what color is and he places his hands on Jonas's back as he says, ". . . Now we must work. And I've thought of a way to help you with the concept of color. Close your eyes and be still, now. I'm going to give you a memory of a rainbow."

The cover of *The Giver* is a beautiful black-and-white photograph that Lowry herself had taken many years before. That picture of an elderly man with his long flowing beard and thoughtful expression is of Carl Nelson. With its perfect title, cover photograph, and thought-provoking plot, *The Giver* began to get a lot of attention.

In a starred review in *The Horn Book Magazine*, the reviewer described Jonas's story by saying, "He learns about war, starvation, neglect, misery, and despair. He learns, to his horror, the truth about the happy release given to old people and newchildren who do not thrive. But he learns also about joys that the community never experiences: they do not see color, or hear music, or know love. . . . The story is skillfully written; the air of disquiet is delicately insinuated. And the theme of balancing the values of freedom and security is beautifully presented."[11]

Even after glowing reviews poured in for *The Giver*, there were still some people who felt it was inappropriate to use in schools. Usually, those people were well-meaning parents who focused on some of the serious issues that were used in telling Jonas's story.

Lowry set up the story to make the reader feel as if Jonas was living in a perfect, almost Utopian world. But, as the story progresses, Jonas begins to understand that not everything is what it seems. When Jonas realizes that euthanasia and infanticide are used to weed out imperfect people in his community, he has a decision to make. Without the use of these ugly, serious issues, there would be no story. Jonas needed those conflicts in order to overcome them and learn.

Speaking about her writing, Lowry has said, ". . . in order for there to be a book, a story, a point, a reason for writing it—the main character makes a journey. Sometimes—very often, in fact, it is an interior journey: a journey that does not involve geography, except the geography of the mind and heart. But there is always a going forth—a quest—a seeking for something—and a coming back, when the something is found."[12]

Even though the serious aspects of *The Giver* were an essential part of Jonas's journey, people still challenged the book. According to the American Library Association, a challenge is an attempt to remove or restrict materials, based upon the objections of a person or group. In 1994, a California school banned the book temporarily after several parents complained about some of its content.[13] Challenges began to pop up all over the country, and *The Giver* got a lot of public attention. It became Lowry's most talked about and controversial book, and in 1994, she was awarded her second Newbery Medal for her efforts.

In her Newbery acceptance speech, Lowry spoke about the many letters she had received from children who had read *The Giver*. "Most of the young readers who have written to me have perceived the magic of the circular journey. The truth that we go out and come back, and what we come back to is changed, and so are we."

Lowry's memories of being "elsewhere" as a shy girl, riding her bike in Tokyo, went into her writing of *The Giver*. And, in an almost unbelievable twist of fate, she experienced her own circular journey because of that book. Her journey began in Shibuya, as she watched the children to whom she was too shy to talk, and it came back full circle the night she accepted her Newbery Medal at the awards banquet.

At the banquet, author and illustrator Allen Say was present to receive the Caldecott Award for his book, *Grandfather's Journey*. Lowry and Say had met several years before the event, and to their surprise, they discovered they had something in common. Lowry told her Newbery audience of the strange coincidence by saying, "Allen was twelve years old when I was. He lived in Shibuya, that alien Elsewhere that I went to as a child on a bicycle. He was one of the Other, the Different, the dark eyed children in blue school uniforms, and I was too timid then to do more than stand at the edge of their school yard, smile shyly, and wonder what their lives were like."[14]

Imagine the buzz that must have spread around the room as the audience realized that the two award winners in front of them had once made eye contact in a foreign land. Listeners were engaged by this revelation, and Lowry impressed them when she spoke directly to Say. "Now I can say to Allen what I wish I could have said then: Watashi-no tomodachi des. Greetings, my friend."[15]

The news of the Lowry and Say reunion spread and became the talk of literary circles for weeks. Some accounts described their discovery as first taking place after Lowry signed a book to Allen and inscribed it in Japanese. From there, they traced their history back to Shibuya and at that point, according to some, Allen then asked Lowry if she was the girl on the green bike.

There is an old saying, "Truth is stranger than fiction," and in the case of Lowry's circular journey, this applies perfectly. Not only did both Lowry and Say become award-winning authors, but they also shared the same editor and publishing house.

Lowry has said that winning her first Newbery in 1990 allowed her to be free to risk failure.[16] Walter Lorraine at Houghton Mifflin took that risk along with her, and in an article for *The Horn Book Magazine*, he wrote, "In an age of conformity Lois is a unique and important voice. She is an author who truly has something to say and is willing to risk saying it. Which is Lois's best book? Certainly *The Giver* is an exceptional book. Still, I am absolutely convinced that Lois's best book is yet to come. I am looking forward to it."[17]

Chapter 9

Magical Gifts and Human Connections

Before 1994 was through, Lowry had several more awards under her belt. *The Giver* was designated as an honor book in the Boston Globe–Horn Book Awards and by The American Booksellers Association. It not only received ten state awards, but was also given an award in Belgium and France—the Le Tam-Tam Award.

For Lowry though, winning awards has not been her most satisfying accomplishment in her writing career. She has said that, "It's in the awareness that reading books makes a difference in the lives of children . . . I think getting people to think about the things that affect our lives is the most important thing, and that's what I will continue to do."[1]

Lowry began connecting with her readers early

on in her career. It is fair to say that Lowry is a person who genuinely cares about children. Her concern for them began long before her career as an author did. As a devoted mother, Lowry postponed her writing aspirations for many years while she nurtured and raised her own children. It was obviously worth the wait.

Since human connections are so important to Lowry, it is nice to think about the fact that as her career grew, so did her family. The addition of grandchildren is just the kind of reward every mother cherishes, and Lowry is no exception to that. By 1995, her children were all grown and off starting their own lives and having families. Her oldest daughter, Alix, had moved to California. Her oldest son, Grey, was living in Germany with his wife and new daughter, Nadine. Lowry's third child, Kristen, lived in Maine with her twelve-year-old son, James. And Benjamin, the youngest of Lowry's four children, lived in Massachusetts.

> **Lowry is a person who genuinely cares about children.**

By this time, Lowry and Martin Small had left their apartment in Boston and relocated to a house in Maine. They still spent time at their home in Massachusetts, but the Maine house allowed Lowry to have two things that were important to her. As a dog lover, she welcomed a shaggy Tibetan terrier into her life and named him Bandit. Moving to Maine also meant Lowry could be closer to her grandchildren. Lowry's grandkids affectionately call her Oma—the German word for grandma.

As with most families, members are brought together during times of celebration and also in times of sorrow. Sadly, this was the case for Lowry's family on a morning in May 1995. Lowry received news that broke her heart. Her son Grey, who was a pilot in the United States Air Force, had died tragically when his plane crashed while flying in formation with another plane.

Lowry flew to Germany for Grey's funeral service, and as she walked with the others and sang *Amazing Grace*, she noticed horses in a meadow nearby. Their manes blew in the wind and Lowry remembered Grey, as a boy, riding his own horse along the river near his boyhood home.

The loss of her son brought back memories of losing her sister. One of the ways Lowry coped with her grief was by having imaginary talks with her mother. They both experienced the loss of a child, and these daydream discussions helped Lowry to look ahead.[2]

Anastasia, Absolutely was in the bookstores and fans found this book to be as charming and funny as the first in the series. This ninth book marked the last book that Lowry has written about her tomboyish character up to this time. But Anastasia's little brother, Sam, still had more adventures to share. Lowry threw her leading character into situations that kept young readers entertained. Only Sam Krupnik would think about running away for not being allowed to wear fangs in his house like he wanted to. But that is just what happened to Sam in 1996 in *See You Around, Sam!* Lowry returned to Sam in 1999 with his fourth book, *Zooman Sam*, making this his last book to date.

Between the Sam books, Lowry stretched the imagination in a book that did not have a human as the main character. Perhaps it was Bandit who inspired her to write about a canine. In *Stay! Keeper's Story*, Lowry introduced readers to a homeless dog who was born in a gutter. Keeper is an endearing pooch with a sophisticated and poetic point of view. His story takes him from master to master until he finds a permanent home. But through homelessness, fame, and family, Keeper always longs for his little sister, Wispy. Lowry's rich language in this tender tale continues to receive praise by those who have read it since its publication in 1997.

Lowry's next book, *Looking Back: A Book of Memories*, was published in 1998. For this book, Lowry used family photographs to compare some of her life's experiences to the creation of her works of fiction. *Looking Back: A Book of Memories* is Lowry's first nonfiction book. Through this autobiography, readers get an eye-opening peek into Lowry's world. The layout is similar to a scrapbook, and her tone is friendly and inviting. The incidents she chose to write about range from laugh-out-loud funny to heart wrenching. By the

Young readers K. Anaïs Peterson (age seven) and M. R. Grant Nishikawa (age four) chat with Lois Lowry in Batavia, Illinois.

end of the book, readers are left feeling as though they have just made friends with this remarkable woman.

Over the years, Lowry has become friends with several popular authors including Katherine Paterson, Phyllis Reynolds Naylor, and Jerry Spinelli, just to a name a few. Even though she does not exchange manuscripts with her writer friends, Lowry has worked with one very good friend for her *Gooney Bird Greene* books. Artist and illustrator Middy Thomas was Lowry's close friend long before they teamed up professionally. They had done a lot of fun and oddball things together, so it was a perfect match when Thomas signed on to illustrate Lowry's books.

Gooney Bird Greene is a humorous story about a second grader who enchants her new classmates with "absolutely true" stories and a most unusual wardrobe. The first book that combined Lowry's words and Thomas's art was released in 2002. The second book, *Gooney Bird Greene and the Room Mother*, did not come out until 2005, but Lowry has future plans for her eccentric little storyteller. She has written the third book and titled it *Fabulous Gooney Bird*, but that may change by the time it goes to print. Speaking about this series, Lowry said, "The first three books are set in October, November, and December, and ideally . . . I will take her through a school year."[3]

Between the publication of the first two Gooney Bird Greene books, Lowry's novel *The Silent Boy* came out. Released in April 2003,

The Silent Boy is set in the early 1900s and tells the story of Katy Thatcher, the daughter of the town doctor. Katy's desire to "know about people" leads to a friendship with Jacob, a farm boy who is mentally challenged. In this book, Katy is grown-up but tells her story as she looks back on her childhood. This is an unusual, and often difficult, point of view for most writers to use, but Lowry does it seamlessly.

For most of her books, Lowry has used limited third person point of view—meaning the story is told by an outside narrator who focuses on one main character. Since *The Giver* was written this way, Lowry used it again when she decided it was time to write the book for which her fans had been begging her. Because the ending of *The Giver* is ambiguous—or left to be understood in more than one way—Lowry was bombarded with letters from readers who wanted a more conclusive ending. When she wrote *The Giver* in 1993, she had no intention of ever writing a sequel. But as years went by and the letters kept pouring in, Lowry found herself asking "what if" questions again.[4] Persistent fans got what they had been asking for when *Gathering Blue* was released in 2000.

For *Gathering Blue*, Lowry set her characters in a future primitive world instead of the Utopian society she had created in *The Giver*. Like Jonas in *The Giver*, Kira, of *Gathering Blue*, also had a magical gift that set her apart from the others. Because *Gathering Blue* tells the story of Kira and does not actually pick up where *The Giver* left off, it is not considered a full-fledged sequel. Instead, it is sold as a companion book due to the fact that Lowry keenly sneaked in a reference to Jonas and hinted to his whereabouts. This tidbit settled many arguments amongst readers of *The Giver*. The ambiguous ending was no more—Jonas's journey now had a conclusion and Kira's story was still unfolding.

In 2004, Lowry unveiled more of Kira's story in *Messenger*. For this book, Lowry gave the main character role to Matty, a boy she first introduced readers to in *Gathering Blue*. In *Messenger*, Matty discovers his magical gift and uses it to bring Kira to his community, known only as Village.

Lowry used her characters from *The Giver* and *Gathering Blue* to skillfully weave their stories together in *Messenger*. Jonas plays a major role in *Messenger* even though Lowry has given him a new title. In *Messenger*, he is simply called Leader. Readers who know Jonas from *The Giver* will recognize him in this scene as he tells Matty how he came to Village:

> Leader laughed. "You've seen the little sled," he said.
> "In the Museum?"
> "Yes. My vehicle of arrival. They've made such a thing of it, it's almost embarrassing. But it is true that I came on that sled. A desperate boy, half dead . . ."

Part of the controversy that surrounded *The Giver* for years was the fact that some readers thought Jonas and his sled-traveling companion, Gabriel, had died at the end. Other readers thought the ending was a happy one, and that is

Lois Lowry at her desk in Cambridge, Massachusetts.

how Lowry thinks of it too. In an interview, she said, "I will say that I find it an optimistic ending. How could it not be an optimistic ending, a happy ending, when that house is there with its lights on and music is playing?"[5]

Lowry was always a little surprised to know that some readers felt that Jonas and Gabriel died in *The Giver*. Clearly though, the controversy about Jonas's whereabouts was put to rest when he reappeared in *Gathering Blue* and *Messenger*. Gabriel even got a small mention in *Messenger*. For Lowry, it was enough to simply let readers know that he had survived and grown into a mischievous boy.

"I did want readers to know that Gabriel was alive and well . . . But I didn't want to focus on an eight-year-old. Could he therefore be used in another book . . . later, when he is older? I suppose there is that possibility."[6] And that possibility has once again sparked readers to write to Lowry. It seems they just cannot get enough of these stories. They now wonder what became of Gabriel, and it is exciting to think about Lowry telling his story.

Connecting with readers has always been important to Lowry, and she once said, "There is something about that moment, when literature becomes accessible, and a door of the world opens."[7] In 2006, *The Worlds of Lois Lowry* invited readers through such a door by combining all three books into a boxed set. *The Giver*, *Gathering Blue*, and *Messenger* are companion books—all related by a common theme and characters that bind them together.

Along with *The Worlds of Lois Lowry*, readers were also invited into another world—the dream world—when Lowry used it for her 2006 novel *Gossamer*. How people affect one another through their relationships is a recurring theme in many of Lowry's novels. *Gossamer* shows how important those human connections are, and it also explores the dream world through a character simply called Littlest One.

> # "When literature becomes accessible . . . a door of the world opens."
>
> **—Lois Lowry**

Littlest One is one of many dream-givers, and her task is to bestow, or give, good dreams to the humans that she has been assigned to. She watches over a seventy-three-year-old woman and an angry young foster child named John.

Gossamer is a fascinating story that reveals how dreams can affect lives just like lives affect dreams. It received great reviews, and *Publishers Weekly* gushed about it by saying, "Lowry's spellbinding story centers on a clever, curious young dream-giver." A reviewer for Kirkus stated, "The prose is light as gossamer; the story as haunting as a dream."

It would not be a surprise if Lowry fans begin writing letters to ask for more stories relating to the characters and story line in *Gossamer*. Her writing is so compelling; it is easy to want more. But Lowry does not discuss her books while she is writing them. She says, "I never talk about my work in progress. It disappears from my imagination if I do."[8]

To keep up with current developments in Lowry's life and career, readers can check her Web site and blog, which she updates regularly. Besides using the World Wide Web to promote her books, she also schedules presentations that take her around the globe. She continues to be a sought-after speaker although she no longer does school visits.

When Lowry is not busy writing or traveling for her speaking engagements, she spends time reading, knitting, gardening, and gathering with friends and family, especially her nine grandchildren. Sadly, she had to say good-bye to her beloved dog, Bandit, when he passed away in the spring of 2006 at the age of twelve. It was not long before Lowry welcomed a new puppy into her life. She had planned to take home a newly born Tibetan terrier, but when she visited the breeder to see the young pups, she spotted three slightly older puppies. After she watched their frolicking antics, Lowry chose the puppy that jumped into a pond and named him Alfie.

Lowry also does a lot of traveling with Martin, and they continue to share a love of music.

Lowry's favorite thing to do in her spare time is watch movies, and she once said, "I would love, if I had to do it over again, to study filmmaking. I would love to make films."[9]

As luck would have it, Lowry did not need to study filmmaking in order to find success in the movie business. *The Giver* is going to be on the big screen. Even though Lowry is not involved with the actual making of the movie, she is in touch with the executives who are.

In addition to this, in 2007 Lois Lowry received the Margaret A. Edwards Award in recognition of her outstanding lifetime contribution of writing for teens. The prestigious award is given by the Young Adult Library Services Association (YALSA), a division of the ALA, and is sponsored by School Library Journal.

Like many of her characters, Lowry, too, has a gift of magical proportions. Her writing has touched the lives of millions and will continue to do so in the future. Readers have followed Lowry through Autumn Street, Elsewhere, Village, and the dream world, and where she takes us next is not yet known. One thing is certain though: Wherever the next journey leads, Lowry is sure to make it memorable.

In Her Own Words

Compiled from e-mail interviews conducted on February 9, 2006, March 9, 2006, and May 1, 2006.

Q: *Your nursery school teacher sent a letter home to your mother stating that, at three years old, your ability to read set you apart from the other children. Tell me about that.*

A: I can actually remember that—the feeling of being set apart. They used to do this thing where they marched around holding their arms like trunks and we were supposed to be elephants. I was supposed to be part of that but this was embarrassing to me. It's weird now thinking of it, that a three year old would feel that way, but I knew I wasn't an elephant. Clearly, that's imaginative play for most children, but I just wanted to sit in a corner and read a book. So, I can see why the teacher said it set me apart.

Q: *Where did your father get the dog tags he had engraved? Were these meant to identify you if you got lost or were they a* token of affection from your father? Do you still have the dog tags?

A: I have had it hanging from a charm bracelet for many years. I'm not sure where my father had them made for my sister and me. They were intended as identification in case New York City was attacked, which seemed a possibility at that time.

Q: What do you remember about the apartment in Brooklyn where you lived as a child? Did you share a room with Helen?

A: It was the first floor of a two-family house. Brick, quite ordinary. Helen and I shared a room; we had bunk beds. Once I was in the upper bunk and she was kicking the springs to jounce me in a kind of game, and a piece of metal fell from the springs into her eye. She had to go to the doctor and it was very scary to me.

Q: How long did you live at your grandparents' house? How old were you when your family moved into their own place not far from your grandparents? Please tell me a bit about that home.

A: We probably lived at my grandparents' for a year, maybe longer, during which my brother was born. Then one half of a two-family house became available for rent, just about five houses away from my grandparents, and we moved there. It was an ordinary house, three bedrooms, and for a while my sister and I shared a room. Then—I'm not sure why; maybe we bickered too much—my mother gave us each our own bedroom, and she shared the master bedroom with my little brother. I loved having my own room; so did Helen.

Q: *Your first fictional piece, "Crow Call," published in Redbook Magazine, was based on a real day of hunting with your father. What did you do with the crows and why were you hunting them?*

A: Crow-hunting was a kind of sport, I think, for guys. I don't recall ever seeing a crow killed and can't imagine what one would do with a dead crow! But it was probably something that outdoorsy guys did in Pennsylvania in the fall.

Q: *Do you use a story plan or an outline for your books?*

A: No, I write by instinct and imagination and impulse. No outlines, no plotting, no plans.

Q: *Tell me about your writing process.*

A: I don't have one. I simply sit at my desk and make up stories and write them down. Then I revise them a little.

Q: *What is your advice to combat writer's block?*

A: The best advice—my only advice—is to sit at one's desk. Butt in chair, hands on keyboard. Fool around with words. Read. I read poetry almost every day because the precision and distillation of language required for poetry is inspiring to me. Some poets more than others, of course. I particularly love the work of Mary Oliver.

Q: *Besides the photographs for The Giver and Number the Stars, what other covers have you done the photographs for?*

A: I did the photographs for the covers of *Gathering Blue* and *Messenger* as well. Of course it is the art director who decides how to use the photo after I take it.

Q: *Have you seen any of the theatrical productions of your books? If so, tell me about that experience.*

A: I've seen the musical and the straight dramatic productions of *Number the Stars*. I've seen a musical of *Anastasia Krupnik*. And I've seen a few scenes from an upcoming production of *The Giver*.

The movie is being done by Walden Media in conjunction with 20th Century Fox. Currently it is in early stages, with the screenplay being tweaked by the director. I've been very privileged that the producers, director, and Jeff Bridges, who is involved, have all consulted with me, sought my opinion about plot details. But it is their project, not mine!

It's always fascinating to see a story I've told move into a different genre, and by necessity take on new, more visual characteristics. And I've loved hearing the music, when they've become musicals! But they become separate from me when they become a theatrical experience. I let go of them.

Q: *What other books have you sold movie or television rights to?*

A: Two books, *Taking Care of Terrific* and *Find a Stranger, Say Goodbye*, were TV movies years ago. *Number the Stars* has been optioned again and again but the film has never been made.

Q: *Tell me about your experiences with censorship and banning of books.*

A: My books are challenged again and again but most often the challenges are handled by the process in place in a school system, and rarely are the challenges ever upheld and the books removed from a school. Sometimes, if a controversy becomes very public, I will be asked to write something for the newspaper, and I'm happy to do that. But the people on the front lines are really the librarians who are always out there fighting for First-Amendment rights.

Q: *Have you ever been verbally attacked or challenged in person?*

A: Yes, occasionally someone who is clearly unstable has called me on the phone, or stood up in an audience (and had to be taken away). But most often I hear from people by letter or e-mail and they are distraught about a book's content—sometimes outraged—but coherent and clearly impassioned. I try always to respect their viewpoint even though I don't agree with it. When it seems appropriate I try to explain why I believe them to be mistaken . . . if, for example, they have not read a book, but have taken things out of context. But I would never take issue with someone's deeply held religious beliefs.

Q: *What do you like to do in your spare time?*

A: I'm a big movie fan . . . I go to a lot of movies . . . and I read voraciously. I like to travel. I knit. I enjoy spending time with friends, family, grandchildren. I love gardens, music, and dogs.

And I am somewhat obsessed by *houses*. I enjoy renovating and remodeling old houses. My house in Maine was built in 1768 and I have loved renovating it so that it's comfortable, pretty, and yet respectful of its own history.

Q: *Where have you traveled for leisure and what is your most memorable trip so far?*

A: I've traveled just about everywhere! All seven continents. I guess one of the most memorable was when I went to Jakarta (Indonesia) to do a week's residency in the international school there; so because I had gone so far, I went on for an additional week, all alone, to west Sumatra to a place called Bukittinggi, which is largely populated by the Minangkabau tribe. I'm fascinated by other cultures and sorry that contemporary world problems make travel less easy, perhaps less safe.

Q: *I love that you were on the television game show Jeopardy! Tell me a little about that.*

A: It was many years ago, in the 70's, when *Jeopardy!* was a daytime show. . . every day, in fact. I did it in order to write an article for the *N.Y. Times* Arts & Leisure section. The producers of the show did not, of course, know I was doing that. I went through the regular procedures to become a contestant. It made a good article . . . it was funny. I lost on the Final Jeopardy question (Sports was the category). I never saw the show because it was live, and before VCRs.

Q: *What is your personal biggest regret?*

A: I have few regrets. I've had a happy and productive life. I wish I had learned to play tennis when I was young! I wish I had asked my parents more questions about their early years—some history is lost when our parents die.

Q: *What would have been your profession if you had not become a writer?*

A: Probably editorial, in publishing. Maybe teaching. Something to do with literature.

Chronology

1937—Lois Hammersberg is born in Honolulu, Hawaii.

1939—The Hammersberg family moves to Brooklyn, New York.

1940—Three-year-old Lois learns to read.

1942—Lois, Helen, and their mother move into her grandparents' home in Carlisle, Pennsylvania.

1943—Lois is allowed to walk to the library alone.

1948—Lois and her siblings move with their mother to Japan.

1950—Lois receives a typewriter from her father for her thirteenth birthday.

1951—The entire Hammersberg family is reunited and lives on Governors Island.

1954—Lois graduates from Packer Collegiate Institute and becomes a college freshman.

1956—At nineteen years old, Lois drops out of college to marry Donald Grey Lowry.

1958—Lois Lowry has her first daughter, Alix.

1959—Lowry's second child, Grey, is born.

1961 Lowry has another daughter, Kristin.

1962—Lowry's fourth child, Benjamin, is born. Her sister, Helen, dies from cancer.

1963—The Lowry family moves to a farmhouse in Portland, Maine.

1972—Lowry graduates from college and is hired to write two textbooks.

1975—Her first piece of fiction, "Crow Call," is published in *Redbook Magazine*.

1977—*A Summer to Die* is published by Houghton Mifflin Publishers; Lowry's marriage ends in divorce.

1978—Lowry is awarded the Children's Book Award by the International Reading Association.

1979—Lowry interviews painter Carl Nelson; Lowry meets Martin Small.

1980—*Autumn Street* is published; Lowry moves to Boston, Massachusetts.

1984—Lowry's fourth Anastasia Krupnik book, *Anastasia, Ask Your Analyst*, is published.

1988—*All About Sam* is published.

1989—*Number the Stars* is published.

1990—Lowry receives her first Newbery Medal for *Number the Stars*.

1993—Lowry and Martin Small buy a house in Maine and get Bandit, a Tibetan terrier; *The Giver* is published.

1994—Lowry receives the Newbery Medal for *The Giver*.

1995—Lowry's son Grey dies in a military plane crash.

1998—*Looking Back: A Book of Memories* is published.

2000—*Gathering Blue*, the companion book to *The Giver*, is published.

2004—The publication of *Messenger* completes *The Giver* trilogy.

2005—The second book in the Gooney Bird Greene series is published.

2006—*Gossamer* is published; Lowry adds a blog to her Web site.

2007—Lowry receives the Margaret A. Edwards Award in recognition of her outstanding lifetime contribution of writing for teens.

Chapter Notes

Chapter 1. Hunting Crows

1. Lois Lowry, "Bright Streets and Dark Paths," Brown University Speech, March 4, 2001, p. 20.
2. Lois Lowry, "Autobiography Feature, Lois Lowry," *Something About the Author* (Thomson Gale, 2002), vol. 127, p. 142.
3. Lowry, "Bright Streets and Dark Paths," pp. 20–22.
4. Personal interview with Melanie Kroupa, March 2006.
5. Lois Lowry, "The Remembered Gate and the Unopened Door," Sutherland Lecture, Chicago Public Library, May 4, 2001, p. 29.
6. IPL Staff, Author Unknown, "Lois Lowry: Frequently Asked Questions," *Internet Public Library Kidspace*, 1996, <http://www.ipl.org/div/kidspace/askauthor/Lowry.html> (December 18, 2005).
7. Lowry, "Autobiography Feature, Lois Lowry," p. 134.
8. Ibid., p. 135.
9. Ibid., p. 137.
10. Ibid.

Chapter 2. The Middle Child

1. Lois Lowry, "How Everything Turns Away," University of Richmond Speech, March 2005, p. 15.

2. Lois Lowry, "Autobiography Feature, Lois Lowry," *Something About the Author* (Thomson Gale, 2002), vol. 127, p. 135.

3. Ibid.

4. Ibid.

5. Lois Lowry, *Looking Back: A Book of Memories* (New York: Houghton Mifflin, Walter Lorraine Books, 1998), p. 67.

6. Ibid., p. 68.

7. Personal interview with Lois Lowry, February 9, 2006.

8. Lowry, *Looking Back: A Book of Memories*, p. 136.

9. Lois Lowry, "The Remembered Gate and the Unopened Door," Sutherland Lecture, Chicago Public Library, May 4, 2001, p. 10.

10. Lowry, "Autobiography Feature, Lois Lowry," p. 138.

11. Lowry, "The Remembered Gate and the Unopened Door," p. 13.

12. Ibid., p. 14.

13. Personal interview with Lois Lowry, February 9, 2006.

14. Lisa Rondinelli Albert, "Lois Lowry: Natural Talent, Magical Gifts, Human Connections," *Children's Writer's and Illustrator's Market* (Cincinnati, Ohio: Writer's Digest Books, 2004), p. 99.

15. Lowry, "Autobiography Feature, Lois Lowry," p. 136.

16. Albert, p. 100.
17. Lowry, "Autobiography Feature, Lois Lowry,"
    p. 136.
18. Ibid.
19. Lowry, "The Remembered Gate and the Unopened
    Door," p. 15.
20. Lowry, *Looking Back: A Book of Memories*, p. 37.
21. Lowry, "Autobiography Feature, Lois Lowry,"
    p. 136.

Chapter 3. On the Move

1. Lois Lowry, "Autobiography Feature, Lois Lowry,"
   Something About the Author (Thomson Gale,
   2002), vol. 127, p. 136.
2. Lois Lowry, "The Remembered Gate and the
   Unopened Door," Sutherland Lecture, Chicago
   Public Library, May 4, 2001, p. 16.
3. Ibid.
4. Lowry, "Autobiography Feature, Lois Lowry,"
   p. 138.
5. Lois Lowry, "Bright Streets and Dark Paths,"
   Brown University Speech, March 4, 2001, p. 2.
6. Ibid.
7. Author unknown, "Merkel Landis," n.d., <http://
   chronicles.dickinson.edu/encyclo/l/ed_landisM.
   htm> (February 21, 2006)
8. Lowry, "Bright Streets and Dark Paths," p. 2.
9. Ibid., p. 3.
10. Ibid., p. 4.
11. Personal interview with Lois Lowry, February 9,
    2006.
12. Lowry, "Bright Streets and Dark Paths," p. 4.
13. Ibid., p. 5.

14. Personal interview with Lois Lowry, February 9, 2006.
15. Lowry, "Bright Streets and Dark Paths," p. 6.
16. Lowry, "The Remembered Gate and the Unopened Door," p. 17.
17. Ibid.
18. Ibid., p. 18.
19. Lois Lowry, "The Beginning of Sadness," Ohio Library Educational Media Association Annual Convention, November 2001, p. 7.
20. Lowry, "Autobiography Feature, Lois Lowry," p. 138.
21. Lowry, "The Remembered Gate and the Unopened Door," p. 32.
22. Lowry, "Autobiography Feature, Lois Lowry," pp. 136–137.
23. Ibid., p. 137.
24. Lowry, "The Remembered Gate and the Unopened Door," p. 24.
25. Lowry, "Autobiography Feature, Lois Lowry," p. 139.
26. Ibid.
27. Diane Telgen, "Autobiography Feature, Lois Lowry," *Something About the Author* (Thomson Gale, 2000), vol. 111, p. 122.
28. Lowry, "Autobiography Feature, Lois Lowry," pp. 138–139.

Chapter 4. The Beginning of Elsewhere

1. Lois Lowry, "Autobiography Feature, Lois Lowry," *Something About the Author* (Thomson Gale, 2002), vol. 127, p. 139.
2. Ibid., pp. 139–140.
3. Ibid., p. 140.
4. Ibid.

5. Ibid.

6. Lois Lowry, "Trade Last," Kerlan Award Speech, April 2004, p. 17.

7. Personal interview with Lois Lowry, February 9, 2006.

8. Ibid.

9. Ibid.

10. Ibid.

11. Lowry, "Trade Last," p. 17.

12. Personal interview with Lois Lowry, March 9, 2006.

13. Lois Lowry, "Newbery Acceptance Speech," June 1994, p. 2.

14. Ibid.

15. Ibid.

16. Lois Lowry, "The Village of Childhood," Children's Literature New England, Vermont, August 1997, p. 1.

17. Ibid., p. 2.

18. Lowry, "Newbery Acceptance Speech," p. 2.

19. Lois Lowry, "How Everything Turns Away," University of Richmond Speech, March 2005, p. 18.

20. Lowry, "Autobiography Feature, Lois Lowry," p. 140.

21. Personal interview with Lois Lowry, February 9, 2006.

22. Lowry, "Autobiography Feature, Lois Lowry," p. 140.

23. Ibid.

24. Lois Lowry, *Looking Back: A Book of Memories* (New York: Houghton Mifflin, Walter Lorraine Books, 1998), p. 99.

25. Ibid.

26. Ibid., pp. 99–100.
27. Lois Lowry, "The Remembered Gate and the Unopened Door," Sutherland Lecture, Chicago Public Library, May 4, 2001, p. 28.
28. Ibid., p. 28.
29. Lowry, "Autobiography Feature, Lois Lowry," p. 140.
30. Ellen Keohane, "Home sweet . . . Governors Isle: Army 'Brats' Recall Island Living," *Downtown Express*, vol. 18, no. 3, June 10–16, 2005, <http://www.downtownexpress.com/de_109/homesweet.html> (March 15, 2006).
31. Lowry, "Autobiography Feature, Lois Lowry," p. 140.
32. Ibid.

Chapter 5. Love, Grief, and Making Trades

1. Lois Lowry, "Autobiography Feature, Lois Lowry," *Something About the Author* (Thomson Gale, 2002), vol. 127, p. 141.
2. Lois Lowry, "Trade Last," Kerlan Award Speech, April 2004, p. 4.
3. Lowry, "Autobiography Feature, Lois Lowry," p. 141.
4. Ibid.
5. Lois Lowry, "Newbery Acceptance Speech," June 1994, p. 3.
6. Lois Lowry, "Bright Streets and Dark Paths," Brown University Speech, March 4, 2001, p. 6.
7. Lowry, "Autobiography Feature, Lois Lowry," p. 141.
8. Ibid.
9. Ibid.
10. Ibid.
11. Ibid.

12. Lowry, "Trade Last," p. 19.

13. Ibid.

14. Lowry, "Bright Streets and Dark Paths," p. 7.

15. Personal interview with Lois Lowry, February 9, 2006.

16. Lois Lowry, autobiographical page, 2002, <http://www.LoisLowry.com/bio.html> (November 22, 2006).

17. Laura M. Zaidman, "Lois Lowry," *Dictionary of Literary Biography* (Detroit: Gale Research Company, 1986), vol. 52, p. 250.

18. Lowry, "Trade Last," p. 22.

19. Ibid., p. 24.

20. Ibid.

21. Author unknown, *"The Giver* Book Notes," n.d., <http://www.bookrags.com/notes/giv/BIO.htm> (March 19, 2006).

22. Lowry, "Bright Streets and Dark Paths, Brown University," p. 18.

23. Shirley Norby and Gregory Ryan, *Famous Children's Authors Book II, Lois Lowry* (Minneapolis: T.S. Denison & Company, 1989), p. 38.

24. Lowry, "Autobiography Feature, Lois Lowry," p. 141.

25. Ibid., p. 142.

26. Ibid.

27. Personal interview with Lois Lowry, February 9, 2006.

28. Personal interview with Melanie Kroupa, March 24, 2006.

29. Personal interview with Lois Lowry, February 9, 2006.

Chapter 6. Journeys of the Heart

1. Lois Lowry, "The Remembered Gate and the Unopened Door," Sutherland Lecture, Chicago Public Library, May 4, 2001, p. 29.
2. Lois Lowry, "Wondering Where Everything Went," National Convention of Teachers of English Annual Convention, Chicago, November 1996, p. 6.
3. Ibid., p. 5.
4. Ibid., p. 7.
5. Ibid.
6. Linda R. Silver, "Review of *A Summer to Die*," *School Library Journal*, May 1977, p. 63.
7. Lois Lowry, *A Summer to Die* (Boston: Houghton Mifflin, 1977), p. 11.
8. Lowry, "The Remembered Gate and the Unopened Door," p. 29.
9. Lowry, "Wondering Where Everything Went," p. 8.
10. Ibid.
11. Walter Lorraine, "Lois Lowry," *Horn Book Magazine*, vol. 70, July/August 1994, p. 427.
12. Lowry, "Wondering Where Everything Went," p. 13.
13. Laura M. Zaidman, "Lois Lowry," *Dictionary of Literary Biography* (Detroit: Gale Research Company, 1986), vol. 52, p. 252.
14. Susie Wilde, "Lois Lowry Interview," *Interview with Lois Lowry BookPage*, 1993, 1998, <http://www.wildewritingworks.com/int/lowrylois.html> (April 2, 2006).
15. Shirley Norby and Gregory Ryan, *Famous Children's Authors Book II*, Lois Lowry (Minneapolis: T.S. Denison & Company, 1989), p. 39.
16. Lorraine, "Lois Lowry," p. 427.
17. Lois Lowry, "Newbery Acceptance Speech," June 1994, p. 4.

18. Author unknown, "An interview with Lois Lowry, 1994 Newbery Medal winner," *The Reading Teacher*, vol. 48, no. 4, December 1994/January 1995, p. 308.
19. Lowry, "Newbery Acceptance Speech," p. 4.
20. Lowry, "Wondering Where Everything Went," p. 13.
21. Lois Lowry, "Autobiography Feature, Lois Lowry," *Something About the Author* (Thomson Gale, 2002), vol. 127, p. 143–144.

Chapter 7. Push a Button

1. Lois Lowry, *Looking Back: A Book of Memories*, First Edition (Boston: Houghton Mifflin, 1998), p. 142.
2. Ibid.
3. Shirley Norby and Gregory Ryan, Famous *Children's Authors Book II*, Lois Lowry (Minneapolis: T.S. Denison & Company, 1989), p. 38.
4. Lois Lowry, "The Remembered Gate and the Unopened Door," Sutherland Lecture, Chicago Public Library, May 4, 2001, p. 32.
5. Lois Lowry, "The Beginning of Sadness," Ohio Library Educational Media Association Annual Convention, November 2001.
6. Personal interview with Lois Lowry, March 9, 2006.
7. Jean W. Ross (interviewer), *Contemporary Authors* (New Revision Series), Linda Metzger, ed., vol. 13 (Detroit: Gale Research Company, 1984), p. 335.
8. Ibid., p. 334.
9. Sally Lodge, "Lois Lowry: Snapshots From Her Life," *Publishers Weekly*, September 7, 1998, p. 29.
10. Lois Lowry, "Autobiography Feature, Lois Lowry," *Something About the Author* (Thomson Gale, 2002), vol. 127, p. 147.

11. Ross, p. 335.

12. Author unknown, "An interview with Lois Lowry, 1994 Newbery Medal winner," *The Reading Teacher*, vol. 48, no. 4, December 1994/January 1995, p. 309.

13. Linda M. Castellitto, "Lois Lowry," *Very Interesting People*, n.d., <http://www.booksense.com/people/archive/lowry.jsp> (April 1, 2006).

14. Lois Lowry, "Wondering Where Everything Went," National Convention of Teachers of English Annual Convention, Chicago, November 1996, p. 3.

15. Lowry, "Autobiography Feature, Lois Lowry," p. 146.

16. Lois Lowry, correspondence to Walter Lorraine at Houghton Mifflin, September 11, 1988, University of Minnesota, Children's Literature Research Collection, Kerlan Collection.

17. Louise L. Sherman, "Book Review," *School Library Journal*, March 1989, p. 177.

18. Lois Lowry, correspondence to Walter Lorraine at Houghton Mifflin, September 11, 1988, University of Minnesota, Children's Literature Research Collection, Kerlan Collection.

19. Lowry, "Autobiography Feature, Lois Lowry," p. 146.

Chapter 8. Full Circle

1. Lois Lowry, "How Everything Turns Away," University of Richmond Speech, March 2005, p. 10.

2. Ibid., p. 11.

3. Ibid., p. 12.

4. Ibid.

5. Lois Lowry, "The Remembered Gate and the Unopened Door," Sutherland Lecture, Chicago Public Library, May 4, 2001, p. 4.

6. Ibid.

7. Lois Lowry, "One Small Thread," Frances Clarke Sayers Lecture, UCLA, May 18, 1997, p. 14.

8. Lois Lowry, "Autobiography Feature, Lois Lowry," *Something About the Author* (Thomson Gale, 2002), vol. 127, p. 147.

9. Lowry, "The Remembered Gate and the Unopened Door," p. 5.

10. Author unknown, "An interview with Lois Lowry, 1994 Newbery Medal winner," *The Reading Teacher*, vol. 48, no. 4, December 1994/January 1995, p. 308.

11. Ann A. Flowers, "Book Review Lois Lowry, *The Giver*," *Horn Book Magazine*, vol. 69, no. 4, July/August 1993, p. 458.

12. Lois Lowry, "Wondering Where Everything Went," National Convention of Teachers of English Annual Convention, Chicago, November 1996, p. 4.

13. Author unknown, *"The Giver," English 240 – Contemporary Children's Literature*, Fall 2000, <http://www.northern.edu/hastingsw/Giver.html> (April 26, 2006).

14. Lois Lowry, "Newbery Acceptance Speech," June 1994, p. 8.

15. Ibid.

16. Ibid.

17. Walter Lorraine, "Lois Lowry," *Horn Book Magazine*, vol. 70, no. 4, July/August 1994, p. 426.

Chapter 9. Magical Gifts and Human Connections

1. Cecelia Goodnow, "The Human Connection Author Strives to Make a Difference in Children's Lives," *Times Union*, May 16, 2004, p. J–4.
2. Lois Lowry, *Looking Back: A Book of Memories*, First Edition (Boston: Houghton Mifflin Company Walter Lorraine Books, 1998), p. 172.
3. Personal interview with Lois Lowry, March 9, 2006.
4. Author unknown, "April 2004: Lois Lowry," *Author Interviews*, p. 30, April 2004, <http://www.downhomebooks.com/lowry.htm> (January 25, 2006).
5. Lois Lowry, *The Giver*, 2nd paperback edition, Walter Lorraine (New York: Dell Laurel-Leaf, 2002), p. 6 of "A Conversation with Lois Lowry" in the back of the book.
6. Author unknown, "April 2004: Lois Lowry," *Author Interviews*, p. 33, April 2004, <http://www.downhomebooks.com/lowry.htm> (January 25, 2006).
7. Ibid., p. 37.
8. Personal interview with Lois Lowry, March 9, 2006.
9. Jean W. Ross (interviewer), *Contemporary Authors* (New Revision Series), Linda Metzger, ed., vol. 13 (Detroit: Gale Research Company, 1984), p. 335.

Glossary

air raid—An attack by hostile aircraft.

Army brat—The child of a career officer of the United States Army.

autobiography—The story of a person's life, written by himself or herself.

banned—To forbid the public distribution of.

blacksmith—A metalworker who shapes iron with an anvil and hammer.

blog—Short for Weblog, a personal online journal.

camaraderie—A feeling of close friendship and trust among a group of people.

compound—An enclosure containing a house, outbuildings, etc.

controversial—Likely to provoke an argument.

darkroom—A room where photographs are developed.

embossed—Having a decorative raised design.

enclave—An enclosed territory that is culturally distinct from the foreign territory that surrounds it.

euthanasia—The act of killing someone painlessly (especially someone suffering from an incurable illness).

evacuate—To withdraw from or vacate a place or area, especially as a protective measure.

foster child—A child in supervised care; usually in an institution or substitute home.

freelance—A person who sells services to employers without a long-term commitment to any of them.

haphazard—Unplanned; happening or done in a way that has not been planned.

hermit—Somebody who chooses to live alone and to have little or no social contact.

immigrants—Newcomers who settle in a country in which they were not born.

infanticide—The act of killing an infant.

introvert—A shy person who tends not to socialize much.

land mines—Explosive devices that are concealed underground.

manuscript—An author's text for a book as it is submitted for publication.

mentor—An experienced supporter who advises and guides a younger, less experienced person.

outline—A rough plan or list of the main points to be covered.

parasol—An umbrella made to provide shade from the sun.

pinafore—A sleeveless dress resembling an apron; worn over other clothing.

precocious—Mature for age.

prestigious—Famous, positively well-known.

prolific—Abundantly productive.

replica—An exact copy of.

reunited—Joined after separation.

sacrifice—A giving up of something cherished or desired for the sake of something else.

savvy—To understand.

stern—Severe, strict.

supplant—To take the place of.

telegram—A message sent by telegraph.

uncanny—Weird, unearthly.

Utopian—Relating to Utopia; an ideally perfect place, especially in its social, political, and moral aspects.

valedictorian—The student with the highest academic rank in a class who delivers the farewell speech at graduation.

Selected Works

Children's Books

1995   *Anastasia, Absolutely*

1996   *See You Around, Sam!*

1997   *Stay! Keeper's Story*

1998   *Looking Back: A Book of Memories*

1999   *Zooman Sam*

2000   *Gathering Blue*

2002   *Gooney Bird Greene*

2003   *The Silent Boy*

2004   *Messenger*

2005   *Gooney Bird Greene and the Room Mother*

2006   *Gossamer*

Textbooks, Articles, and Short Stories

1973   *Black American Literature*, textbook

1974   *Literature of the American Revolution*, textbook

"How Does It Feel to Be on a TV Quiz Show? Don't Ask," *The New York Times*

1975   "Crow Call," *Redbook Magazine*

"Picturing Children as They Really Are," *The New York Times*

"The Colonial Life at Strawberry Banke," *The New York Times*

"Remembering How It Was," *The Writer*

2000   "Future Classics," *The Horn Book Magazine*

Further Reading

Books

Chaston, Joel D. *Lois Lowry*. Twayne's United States Authors Series. Independence, Ky.: Twayne Publishers, 1997.

Hill, Christine M. *Ten Terrific Authors for Teens*. Berkeley Heights, N.J.: Enslow Publishers, Inc., 2000.

Lowry, Lois. *Looking Back: A Book of Memories*. New York: Houghton Mifflin Publishers, 1998.

Internet Resources

Lois Lowry's Web site
   http://www.loislowry.com

"Lois Lowry," teenreads.com
   http://www.teenreads.com/authors/au-lowry-lois.asp

"Lois Lowry," Kidspace @ The Internet Public Library
   http://www.ipl.org/div/kidspace/askauthor/Lowry.html

Index

92
LOW

Albert, Lisa Rondine
Lois Lowry : the
giver of stories and
memories

DEC   2008

DATE DUE